Courtesy of Bob McGill © 2012 Shutterbug Atlanta

*Courtesy of Ray Leader, Federal Aviation Administration (Retired), Hartsfield-Jackson Atlanta International Airport.
Atlanta Airport (circa 1920's)*

What's In A Name?

A Historical Perspective of
Hartsfield-Jackson
Atlanta International Airport
1925 - 2014

Dale Hartsfield

What's In A Name?
A Historical Perspective of Hartsfield-Jackson Atlanta International Airport 1925-2014
Copyright © 2014 by Dale Hartsfield

www.hartsfieldspeakers.com
www.dalehartsfield.com

All rights reserved solely by the author. The author guarantees
all contents are original and do not infringe upon the legal rights
of any other person or work. No part of this book may be reproduced
in any form without the permission of the author. The views expressed
in this book are not necessarily those of the publisher.

Printed in the United States of America
Editor & Designer
Donna Garrison Leonard
www.leonardodesigns.net

ISBN-9781505400274
History / Atlanta / Airports

Cover Photos:
Courtesy of the Atlanta Hartsfield-Jackson International Airport
Courtesy of Bob McGill © 2012 Shutterbug Atlanta

About the Author
Dale Hartsfield

Dale Hartsfield is a native of Atlanta. He grew up in south Atlanta near the airport. He loves public speaking and teaching. His first "paid" speaking event occurred in 1984. Since he was nineteen, he has been teaching, primarily in churches. He enjoys speaking at both Christian and secular events. Although, he is far from perfect, he strives to live his life according to his strong beliefs and principals, such as integrity, high moral ethics and character. His credible story telling is a learning experience combined with education, suspense and humor.

Dale loves God first, his family, friends and country. His life demonstrates his beliefs. Dale and his wife, Amy, have two children and seven grandchildren. He is a veteran of the United States Marine Corps and received his Business Communications degree from Kennesaw State University at age forty. He also attended Georgia Southern University and Atlanta Christian College.

In 2003, Dale was the family spokesman for the Hartsfield family when the city of Atlanta renamed the airport. Although not an author, the controversy prompted Dale to write **What's in a Name?** He therefore, dedicates this book to the memory of Mayor William Berry Hartsfield.

Courtesy of the Atlanta Hartsfield-Jackson International Airport

Forwards

MAYOR SAM MASSELL
Mayor of Atlanta, 1970 - 1974
President Buckhead Coalition, 1988 - current

As a native Atlantan in my eighty-sixth year, the reader can imagine I've got a good recollection of much of this City's growth, including its introduction to aviation. I even remember the first little yellow-brick terminal my dad took me to see. Add to this my twenty-two years in various elected offices, including four as its Mayor, and one can well understand my knowledge and appreciation of the changes I've witnessed.

I open with this credential allowing me to endorse Dale Hartsfield's writings, which give a thorough introduction to how aviation evolved in Atlanta, with a new stage in its development added yearly. When you consider that we have had management by nine mayors over these years, we can acknowledge that once Mayor William B. Hartsfield exercised his interest in this field, every successor added to part of its expansion, both in physical size and technological improvements.

Although Dale spends considerable effort explaining how and why the many name changes of our airport have taken place, the book is much more than just naming rights, and is really a history book on what, when, why, who, and where. It happens I am mostly interested in the naming portion of this work, because of my own involvement in naming the Atlanta airport, and my philosophy about "naming" in general.

Yes, as this book reports, when Mayor Hartsfield passed away, I was Mayor, and promptly urged City Council, then called the Board of Aldermen, to name our airport in his honor. It might be interesting to know that without his approval and while he was still in life, we named an old city incinerator for him which he did NOT appreciate. As Mayor Maynard Jackson was the one who was my opponent in 1973, it was appropriate that when he passed away and the idea to use his name on the airport was proposed, my opinion wasn't solicited. I stayed out of that controversy, but admit I was surprised that after Mayor Franklin asked a Blue Ribbon Committee she had appointed to make a recommendation, she didn't follow their conclusion.

Incidentally, I have long had a position that public property should not be named for persons still in life. This has been my answer when City Councilmen and other well-meaning citizens have suggested some naming honor to me, I have rejected it with this philosophy. Although the reason is not that one airport in a southern city removed a civic leader's name from its airport when the person was sentenced to jail for wrongdoing. I just believe there are too many situations that could cause regret.

Dale would probably not know this, but Mayor Hartsfield collected rocks, and a few of us (Margaret MacDougal, Ada Toombs, and Helen Bullard) used the code word "Rocky" when we didn't want people to know who we were discussing. I found that being called "Buddy" until going to college because I was a "Jr.", was confusing as a political candidate. For this reason, when I had a son, I named him Steve Alan Massell so he didn't have to have a nickname, but his initials spelled SAM.

For the past twenty-five years, I have been managing a nonprofit civic group, focusing our mission on the quality of life in the community of Buckhead. In doing so, I've had to struggle with the name Buckhead. It is not only an odd moniker, but whereas we are only a forty-four-neighborhood Community in the City of Atlanta, just about sixty miles east of here exists an actual incorporated (200 population) city named Buckhead, and when Atlanta hosted the Olympics, the kiosk at Atlanta's airport that intended to help visitors find their way, caused considerable confusion when people entered the destination, "Buckhead".

For that matter, it takes careful effort to be certain what we chamber-boosters mean when we boast about growth and other achievements of "Atlanta", for the City of Atlanta has only some 450,000 residents, whereas many reports record a population for "Atlanta" around six-million (when what is meant is "Metro" Atlanta).

As this book admits, much of our history is being erased as city streets and other public property is being renamed, by adding the identification of Atlanta's "new" leaders, mostly from the African-American community, in place of earlier City Fathers. In this vein, I actually made a speech to an Hispanic association a couple of years back, predicting that the growth in the Latin Community would probably lead to many public places being re-named for them in some fifty years.

Sometimes it's more than the names that change. Reference is made herein to "Willie B", the gorilla at Atlanta's zoo named for our Mayor Hartsfield. It was as popular as our Mayor, and I mean that in its most truthful way. But, I was saddened to know that a hippopotamus named for me at the zoo died because, according to the then zoo director, "it could not reproduce", 'tho this doesn't sound like reason enough to give one's life.

I have been very impressed with the proficiency with which our airport managers over the years have run this gigantic facility, even though it always seems to be controversial. I knew several of them, but George Berry, serving under Mayor Jackson, was the one with whom I had the closest relationship. He ran my term as Mayor and made me look good. I was equally impressed with the magnitude of how much changes cost, in the many millions, for instance when a runway had to be made longer to accommodate one type of plane, and then deeper, instead, to handle the thrust of another brand; or the cost to better manage simultaneous landings and takeoffs to fit new FAA regulations changed overnight.

George was the one who helped us arrange the purchase of the 10,000 acres in Dawson/Forsyth as a "potential" future second airport, which served the immediate purpose of satisfying the daily press that it seems every seven years calls for another airport, which doesn't work well for Delta, and this airline is the lifeblood of our City's operation.

The reader will find that the Mayors of yesteryear all had the same problems, crime, traffic, the economy; and even the suggestion that a better partnership needed to be developed between the City of Atlanta and the County of Fulton, just like Mayor Kasim Reed called for in his second inauguration speech this January 2014.

I've benefitted from good relationships with many Atlanta Mayors, most especially Bill Hartsfield. For this reason alone, I'm very pleased to be part of this book.

DICK YARBROUGH
Syndicated Columnist, www.dickyarbrough.com

Dale Hartsfield has reminded us of what a difference a visionary can make. In this case, that visionary happens to be his relative, former Atlanta Mayor William B. Hartsfield, the city's longest-serving mayor who held reign from 1937 to 1961, except for a short time after his first term.

Perhaps that name is familiar to you in another way: He is the "Hartsfield" in the world's busiest airport, Hartsfield-Jackson. That is a fitting tribute. Had it not been for the vision of Mayor Hartsfield, you might be flying out of Birmingham these days.

Dale Hartsfield has put together a compelling account of how the Atlanta airport was transformed from the Quonset Hut of my childhood to the magnificent and sometimes maddening facility it is today and how a city that doesn't always appreciate its history, came close to changing the airport's name in a rush to honor Atlanta's first African-American mayor. Fortunately, that story has a happy ending.

What's in a Name? is a story of our past, our present and our future. It is the story of what one man can do when he sees something the rest of us don't see: the future.

MIKE LINCH
Senior Pastor, North Star Church

I have had the privilege to know Dale Hartsfield and his family for the past twenty years. I know this about Dale: he has a love for his family, a love for his Lord and a love for his city. You will discover in these pages, the story behind one of the most iconic names in Atlanta "Hartsfield" and why this name means so much to Dale. Enjoy the journey through this journey of ***What's In A Name?***.

DR. DWIGHT "IKE" REIGHARD
President/CEO MUST Ministries, Senior Pastor Piedmont Church

When I am returning from a long trip on an airplane there is no sweeter sound than hearing the flight attendant announce, "We would like to welcome you to Atlanta's Hartsfield-Jackson International Airport." There are, in fact, very few family names that are more synonymous with the City Of Atlanta than that of the Hartsfield Family.

Dale Hartsfield, a distant cousin of the legendary Mayor of Atlanta, William B. Hartsfield, has spent nearly five years in research for his book on the Hartsfield Family, and the names of the world's busiest airport. It has been a labor of love and privilege for Dale to bring to life the story of his family history through the lens of a family member.

Growing up in downtown Atlanta, I remember Mayor Hartsfield as the one that fostered Atlanta's image as, "the city too busy to hate." He is one of the greatest Mayors in Atlanta's long history, and helped to usher in Atlanta as an international city with the expansion of the airport which bears his name. No Mayor served longer than Atlanta native, William B. Hartsfield, and no one did more to raise the profile of Atlanta in the 1940 & 1950's than the Mayor.

You will enjoy an insider's look at the family and legacy through the pages of Dale's very first book. I hope you will be as blessed as I was in reading the story of the family that helped to shape my beloved City Of Atlanta!

Courtesy of Bob McGill © 2012 Shutterbug Atlanta

Acknowledgements

What's In A Name? was only possible due to the help and encouragement of many people. I am not a writer, but I did have a story to tell.

Above all else, I want to thank my God, my Savior Jesus Christ, and the Holy Spirit, for the strength and ability to write my story.

Second, I want to thank my wife, Amy, and my children, Carey and Walt, for their support, although they all thought I was crazy for taking on this task.

Dana Herron, Tiffany P. Clevenger and C. H. Smith helped me with the initial edits in the beginning stages. Donna Leonard, with Leonardo Designs, helped with writing, final editing, content development, layout, photos, cover design and final completion. Without Donna and her design commitment, this book would not have been possible.

Ulysses "Simpson" Simmons was a colleague at the ***Atlanta Journal,*** and the first person that suggested I write a book, even before Jackson's name was added to Hartsfield. After the airport name was changed, he suggested that I turn the Jackson chapter upside down to make it controversial.

Many people encouraged me along the way to press on and finish the book. There were some difficult days during the writing process, and I almost quit a few times as life got in the way.

I have to thank many friends including my best buddy, Hank Chandler, whom I've known since the airport was named Hartsfield in 1971. Eddie Williams, Dr. Joe Teal, Alice Hughes (whose mother was a Hartsfield), and Mayor Hartsfield's grandson, Monty Cheshire, encouraged me immensely.

Special thanks to Mayor Sam Massell, Dick Yarbrough, Pastor Mike Linch, and Dr. Ike Reighard for writing forwards. Big thanks to Bob McGill, my photographer and Chris Ward, my webmaster. Thanks to Chris Boggess for helping with video on my web site.

I received continuous encouragement from my sisters Gail Hartsfield McKinney, and Marsha Hartsfield Hendricks. Both sisters helped with various things during the writing process.

Others who encouraged me included: Pastor Dr. Dewey Davidson, friends Ken Crocker, Joe Herrington, Steve Reece, Larry Robinson, Earl Styes, Gerry Rogers, Jim Mullen, Tim Gowens, Scott Falconer, Bill Fowler, Doug Moore, Joel Anderson, Pastor Robert Ledbetter, Pam Smith, Andy Duncan and my many Chick-Fil-A Brookstone friends, my cousin Connie Appling, Dr. Jean Molinary, Mary Durueke, Stacy Cook, Andy Russell, Bob Millinor, Murray Farquhar. Grant Wainscott and Ray Leader (retired FAA) from the National Aviation Museum, Kenn Kington, Dennis Deal, (cousin of Governor Nathan Deal), Betsy and John Braden (Betsy was the co-author of ***A Dream Takes Flight***), Kathleen Bergen of the FAA (who helped set up pictures at the FAA Atlanta tower), Ken Mcconahay, my tour guide at the FAA tower at Hartsfield-Jackson. Jeff Adams, Allen Hardage, Sammy Davis, Mark Smith, Sylvia O'Neal and Myrna White from Hartsfield-Jackson, George Berry, a former airport manager, my Ford accessory customers, Bill Miller, Rusty Stewart, John Blankenship, Craig Cook, Richard Smith, David Ellis, Ed Hooker, Scott Thounhurst, Jason Anderson and Jennifer Kasper, from Xulon Press.

What's In A Name? would not have been possible without the support and encouragement of friends and family! Thank you!

Courtesy of Bob McGill © 2012 Shutterbug Atlanta. Delta concourses at Hartsfield-Jackson Atlanta International Airport

Courtesy of Bob McGill © 2012 Shutterbug Atlanta. Delta concourses at Hartsfield-Jackson Atlanta International Airport

Contents

1 **What's In A Name?** 21

2 **Who's Hartsfield?** 31

3 **The History Of An Airport** 63

4 **Atlanta Has A History of Changing Names** 119

5 **2003** 129

6 **The Jackson Era** 157

7 **Facts, Figures & Future** 177

Left Photo: Courtesy of Ray Leader, Federal Aviation Administration (Retired), Hartsfield-Jackson Atlanta International Airport. 1939 control tower at Atlanta Airport (circa 1940's)

Introduction

After the 2003 name change of the Atlanta airport, I wondered, "Why has the name changed five times in less than 100 years?" What were the reasons behind all the name changes? Through the years there were many different city officials who had the opportunity to make a name change and they did. Why did they feel it was necessary to make any change? In my book, I explore the many facets of these decisions. From my perspective, I attempt to unravel the story behind this great airport. I hope you will conclude with my personal opinion, that the airport should have remained named solely for Mayor William B. Hartsfield.

Hartsfield was a city alderman when the airport was first named Candler Field. He was the Mayor of Atlanta when it was named Atlanta Municipal Airport. After his death, I believe it was rightfully renamed for William B. Hartsfield, for he was known as the "father of aviation" in Atlanta.

Courtesy of Ray Leader, Federal Aviation Administration-Retired, Hartsfield-Jackson Atlanta International Airport. CandlerField/Atlanta Airport (circa 1920's)

I was certainly disappointed after the 2003 name change. In looking for historical accounts of the airport, I was surprised by the limited amount of information that was publicly accessible. In my research, I found one book about the world's busiest airport that was extremely helpful. It is ***A Dream Takes Flight*** written by Betsy Braden and Paul Hagan.

A Dream Takes Flight thoroughly chronicles the airport history, including the history of aviation in the south and Atlanta, particularly from 1910 till 1980. I encourage you to read it as it is an in-depth history book on aviation. I found it to be an excellent resource during my hundreds of hours of research. However, it ended in the year 1980. To my knowledge, there has not been another book written about the Atlanta airport that has continued to present day.

What's In A Name? will highlight Atlanta's airport history without going into as much depth as ***A Dream Takes Flight.*** My intent is to provide an overview of the airport's history, including it's name changes, and how the name Hartsfield has been an integral part in three of the airports names.

William B. Hartsfield was also instrumental in the earlier names, Candler Field and Atlanta Municipal Airport.

I admit I am a little biased about the airport name. Obviously, you would expect that! However, I have tried to do everything I possibly can to be fair and honest about the history, including Mayor Hartsfield and Mayor Jackson.

What's In A Name? also touches on the importance of names for people and places. In 2003, when the airport name change was proposed, I began to research and review information about William B. Hartsfield, my distant relative, and about his involvement with the City of Atlanta and the airport. The title of my book ***What's in A Name?*** reflects on how we name things and how important those names become to us.

Although I wanted to write a book about the history of this great airport, I also wanted it to be a fun read, not a boring history, so I started out with the chapter of how we name everything.

I had not expected that writing the book would be as difficult and time consuming, considering what I already knew about the airport's history. After the 2003 name change to Hartsfield-Jackson, I started contemplating this story and began writing in the fall of 2008. It took me a while to complete, because "life" kept getting in the way!

I underestimated this project, however, it was a lot of fun and very rewarding. I trust you will also enjoy learning about the rich and varied history of the Hartsfield-Jackson Atlanta International Airport.

Courtesy of Bob McGill © 2012 Shutterbug Atlanta. Present day Hartsfield-Jackson Atlanta International Airport

Courtesy of the Atlanta Hartsfield-Jackson International Airport. At the opening of the 5th runway in May 2006, Steve Penley's painting was unveiled

Chapter One

What's In A Name?

Courtesy of Ray Leader, Federal Aviation Administration (Retired), Hartsfield-Jackson Atlanta International Airport. Atlanta Airport (circa 1940's)

STOP! The lady yelled at me as she came out of her apartment. "What is your name?" she yelled as she approached me. As a twelve year old boy, I knew it was time to run. Why did she want to know my name? What was the problem? I would be in trouble if she found out my name, so maybe to avoid those consequences, it was best if I tried to run, so I did.

At this point in my life my name was important, at least to her. I was hoping she would not find out my name. This short story has nothing to do with Atlanta's airport, but it does have something to do with ***What's In A Name?!***

I had gone swimming in the apartment pool behind our house. Of course, I wasn't supposed to

Courtesy of the Atlanta Hartsfield-Jackson International Airport (circa 1940's)

be there. My parents had already warned me not to go swimming in that pool. I was with my twin sister, Gail, and my friends Scott and Mike Bailey. We had been diving for marbles in the pool. I don't remember exactly what happened, but Scott made me mad, and I ran after him into the street behind the pool. I threw one of the marbles at him. Oops! I missed Scott, but threw a perfect curve ball. The marble flew directly into a Cadillac windshield. My timing was perfect. The lady who owned the car had just come out of her apartment, and now she wanted my name.

We all ran, but she kept close enough to see the direction we all headed. She asked some other children about us, and they told her our names and where we lived. Now that she had my name, I was certainly in big trouble.

Later that day, a police car showed up at our house. My father told the officers that he would certainly take care of the matter. In addition to weeks of restriction, I remember paying for that windshield over the next several months. Looking back, I know that my father making me pay for the windshield was not just a matter of making amends, but more importantly, it was also his way of keeping our name respectable. The neighborhood knew the Hartsfield family would take responsibility for their actions. They knew the Hartsfield family would treat people fairly and repay a debt owed. Once the woman knew my name, my name had to be restored along with the windshield.

one's name is more important than silver or gold

The Bible tells us, the reputation of one's name is more important than silver or gold (Proverbs 22:1). Whether a personal name, name of a business, or name of an airport, obviously, names are important.

I grew up in a mostly white, middle-class neighborhood in metro Atlanta. I was born in Marietta, a suburb of Atlanta. As a child, we moved to the City of East Point. East Point was within the shadow of what was becoming one of the world's busiest airports. My father worked for Delta Air Lines, which was the major reason for the move. Most people identify Delta Airlines with the Atlanta airport.

Delta and Eastern were the major airlines in Atlanta, from the 1940's through early 1990's, before Eastern ceased operations. Their demise was directly related to the machinist union strike which began March 1989. It was a very bitter labor dispute, and along with surging aviation fuel prices, the airlines was forced out of business on January 18, 1991. [1]

When the former mayor of Atlanta, William Berry Hartsfield, died in 1971, I started paying more attention to the airport because of my name. Hartsfield's death brought about enormous media coverage remembering his service to Atlanta and his numerous accomplishments.

At that time, I was a thirteen year old student at Briarwood High School in East Point. Until that

1. NY Times.com Archives, January 20,1991, By Agis Salpukas

moment, I didn't grasp what his death would mean to me in the future. Also, I didn't know much about William Berry Hartsfield. I knew we were distant relatives and that seemed like something that might help a young man out, especially trying to meet girls. I began to introduce myself as Dale Hartsfield, "Hartsfield like the airport." That introduction got people's attention. I still introduce myself that way. Growing up as a Hartsfield in the Atlanta area certainly had some advantages.

As I got a little older, I began to have fun with my name. Even as the metro Atlanta area population exploded, most people especially the younger ones, had no idea why the airport was named Hartsfield. I used this to my advantage. As I began to date, I would often tell girls that my daddy owned the airport. Sometimes, they would ask me, "what airport?" Other times they would say, "Really!" which caused them to become very interested in me. That line did get me a few dates through the years.

Looking back, I realize that a lot of people did not know much about local and national history. I could not blame the girls for not knowing about Mayor Hartsfield, because as I said I didn't know much

Courtesy of Bob McGill © 2012 Shutterbug Atlanta

Courtesy of Ray Leader, Federal Aviation Administration (Retired), Hartsfield-Jackson Atlanta International Airport. Aerial view of Candler Racetrack which became the Atlanta Airport (circa 1920's)

about him, even though I was a Hartsfield. As an adult, I now understand how important our history, our names and our heritage are.

Many people did not know much about Hartsfield because they had migrated into the Atlanta area after his time as mayor. Others knew little about his accomplishments at the airport or in the City of Atlanta, partly due to a lack of history being taught in public schools. History often bores young people, but as we age, we begin to realize the value of our history.

History reveals and reflects the meaning and importance of names. Everything and every person is recognized by a given name. Names identify us as individuals and as families. Names are used to identify businesses, places or even airports, which can often memorialize a significant person.

Webster's dictionary defines a name as a word or phrase that constitutes the distinctive designation of a person or a thing. People began to use descriptions that would ultimately transform to surnames or last names so they could distinguish one from another.

In the thirteenth century, most males were named John, William or Richard, according to an on-line source, so if someone mentioned a person named John in conversation, that person had to explain which John he was referring to. [2] He might say "John, the son of Andrew," or he might say "John, the cook." These descriptions would later become surnames, such as Anderson and Cook. Last names are important because they connect us to our past: our ancestors and our heritage.

2. www.behindthename.com/surnames

Your last name gives you a sense of identity and helps you discover who you are and where you come from.[3] Some names are represented by the family Coat of Arms and Family Crests.

The name Hartsfield is an Americanized form of Harzfeld, an Ashkenazic Jewish ornamental name formed with German Harz + Feld 'field'. [4]

This is not a religious book, but in the Bible, in the old and new testaments, names were important to God. In Genesis, the first book of the Bible, God gave Adam the responsibility of naming all the beasts of the field and the birds of the air. In Genesis 1:19, God brought every living creature to Adam and whatever Adam called them, that became their names.

In the New Testament, the book of Matthew starts out with the lineage of Jesus Christ. Matthew 1:21, says that Mary would bring forth a son and that his name would be called Jesus, meaning Savior.

God, Himself, is referred to by many different names which reveal His character. In the Bible, men and women's names were also used to describe things about their character and nature.

Controversy exists today, as it always has from the beginning, over the mention of the name of Jesus. I believe in the name of Jesus and won't apologize or downplay my beliefs. I have always stood for whatever I believed was right, which is why I fought to maintain the name of Hartsfield at the Atlanta airport. As you continue reading **What's in a Name?**, you will see why I continue to stand for the Hartsfield family name.

How important is your name? Does your name matter? Is it significant? What about famous names? If you have someone famous in your family, you proudly tell others about that person. That is the case with me when I talk about a famous relative named William Berry Hartsfield.

Most people recognize names of great places like the Grand Canyon, State of Alaska or Niagra Falls. Despite our problems, I believe we live in the greatest country in the world. When I hear the

3. www.ancestry.com, pg. 1
4. www.ancestry.com/hartsfield

Courtesy of Dale Hartsfield, 2014
Varsity on Spring Street, another great Atlanta landmark name

Chapter 1 - What's In A Name?

Courtesy of Ray Leader, Federal Aviation Administration (Retired), Hartsfield-Jackson Atlanta International Airport. Atlanta Airport (circa 1970's)

name, "The United States of America," I feel proud and honored. I think of all the men and women who have died to protect our name and give us our freedom. I believe this nation is worth fighting for. We should all be appreciative and thankful for our country.

What about nicknames? In high school, I had friends named Binky, Deiter and Goober! We always called them by those nicknames. Everyone probably knows some people who have strange and interesting names. I have a friend named Moby, who is a radio announcer in Atlanta, whose real name is James. Many Atlantans might recognize his nickname.

In addition to the Atlanta Airport, there are other names that put Atlanta on the map. One famous name is **Gone with the Wind,** authored by Margaret Mitchell, another famous Atlantan. Also, Stone Mountain and Kennesaw Mountain are known as historical civil war landmarks.

you will eventually drive down a street named Peachtree

We have names for everything. If you are driving in Atlanta, you will eventually drive down a street named Peachtree. There are numerous streets that include the name Peachtree. Auburn Avenue often referred to as "Sweet Auburn," is another famous street in Atlanta.

Right Photo: Courtesy of the Atlanta Hartsfield-Jackson International Airport. Interchange near the airport

Courtesy of Ray Leader, Federal Aviation Administration (Retired), Hartsfield-Jackson Atlanta International Airport. Atlanta Airport (circa 1980's)

Smyrna, Marietta, East Point, Tucker, Roswell, Alpharetta, Lithonia and Jonesboro are some interesting local city names.

Coca Cola, Home Depot, UPS, Delta and Chick-Fil-A are some famous local businesses in the Atlanta area. Some names give us a clue as to what they do, like Georgia Power. Another major corporation that was adjacent to the Atlanta airport for many years, was the Atlanta Ford Assembly Plant. These major corporations are names we all recognize. Some names stand for something that we may have forgotten. WSB is one of Atlanta's local radio and TV stations. Originally it stood for, "Welcome South Brother."

Turner Field was named for long-time Braves owner Ted Turner. The origins of other names may have been forgotten, which seems to be the case for Hartsfield International Airport.

Centennial Olympic Park is a well-chosen name. In 2003, some pushed along with me, to add Maynard Jackson's name to the park, because he was the mayor that brought the Olympics to Atlanta. I thought that would be appropriate since it would not have replaced or hyphenated an existing name.

I am not only a Hartsfield, but I am also proud of the fact that I am an American, an Atlantan, a Georgian, a former U.S. Marine, and a Christian.

During my childhood, my parents received a lot of mail that was addressed to Mr. John or Mr. Johnny Hartsfield. That presented a problem, that was not my father's name. My mother's name was Johnnie, a southern female name. If that was not bad enough, her middle name was Hortense. She did not like being known as Johnnie Hortense Hill, and was more than happy to take on the Hartsfield name, Mrs. Johnnie H. Hartsfield. My father,

James Harold Hartsfield, was a man of integrity who did what he said and was greatly respected by everyone. He was an extremely wise man and will always have a special place in my heart.

A lot of similar objects or products can be called by different names. For example, I drink soft drinks. A soft drink can be referred to as a pop, soda pop, or fountain drink. In the south, we just call it a coke! Coca Cola IS THE Atlanta drink. Sorry, Pepsi.

In my book, *What's In A Name?*, I attempt to give a historical account from my perspective. I expound on the names of the Atlanta airport and their origins. The history of the world's busiest airport is as complex and diverse as the millions of people that pass through it every year.

Courtesy of Dale Hartsfield, Mar. 1966, Vacation flight with Dale's family

Courtesy of Dale Hartsfield, Mar. 1966, Vacation flight with Dale's family

Chapter 1 - What's In A Name?

Courtesy of Dale Hartsfield, 2014, Coca-Cola Building, Atlanta, Georgia

Chapter Two
Who's Hartsfield?

William Berry Hartsfield was Atlanta's longest serving mayor and known as the "father of aviation" in Atlanta. The Atlanta airport has been passive in preserving and promoting the memory of W. B. Hartsfield. Before 2003, most people did not know who the airport was named for or what part W. B. Hartsfield played in bringing the airport to Atlanta. In today's fast paced world, there is a lack of attentiveness to the history of W. B. Hartsfield and the airport, which is why I am writing this book.

People ask how I am related to the Mayor. My answer is always: distantly. I certainly am not a "kissing cousin." Actually, I am a fourth or by some accounts a fifth cousin. I never met the Mayor, but growing up I remember my dad and other relatives talking about him often.

The next question often asked is "Why do you speak about and promote the former mayor and the airport as you do"? Personally, I have been introducing myself as "Hartsfield like the airport," since it was originally named for Hartsfield in 1971. Even though there were not a lot of relatives still alive, there were a few, including myself, who were willing to take on the City of Atlanta in a battle concerning the name of the world's busiest airport.

The closest living relative to Mayor Hartsfield is Monty Cheshire, his grandson. Monty resides with his family in Macon, Georgia. I spoke with Monty on several occasions during the 2003 airport name change. I did not have the pleasure of meeting him until I started writing this book. His input has been invaluable. Monty contributed many of the Hartsfield family photos that he found in his mother's

Courtesy of the Atlanta Hartsfield-Jackson International Airport. Mayor W. B. Hartsfield.

attic after her passing in 2012. She was buried near her father, William B. Hartsfield in Atlanta. Monty shared his personal insight with me regarding his relationship with his grandfather, Mayor W. B. Hartsfield.

William Berry Hartsfield was quite simply one of the most famous persons in Atlanta history. He was born March 1, 1890, on Butler Street, near the present day Grady Memorial Hospital. He was the son of Charles Green Hartsfield and Victoria Dagnall Hartsfield. Early on, he was called Willie.

Courtesy of Monty Cheshire, grandson of W. B. Hartsfield. Hartsfield at one year old

Charles, his father, moved the family to the Grant Park area of town in 1902. (Later in 1959, The Atlanta Zoo at Grant Park, named their baby gorilla, Willie B., after Mayor Willie B. Hartsfield.)

Willie attended Boy's High in Atlanta but dropped out of school in his senior year so he could attend Dixie Business School in the evenings. He felt that learning about business was more important than a formal education. As a young person, Hartsfield had a friend who shared his views on education. That boyhood buddy was Robert Woodruff.

"In 1919, a group of investors headed by Ernest Woodruff and W. C. Bradley purchased the Coca-Cola Company for $25 million. Four years later, Robert Winship Woodruff, Ernest Woodruff's son, was elected president of the company, beginning more than six decades of active leadership in the business." [1]

Willie and Robert's friendship began between the two young men in their childhood and lasted throughout their lives. Woodruff's faith in Hartsfield as an honest man, full of integrity, never failed as Hartsfield moved into his political career. Hartsfield, in turn, always sought his friend, Woodruff, for counsel and support on matters concerning the welfare of Atlanta.

"As Woodruff moved on with greater and greater success in the business world, from the Ice and Coal Company to the White Truck Company, and from there to the beginning

1. www.thecoca-colacompany.com/heritage

Courtesy of Monty Cheshire, grandson of W. B. Hartsfield. (from left to right) W. B. Hartsfield's parents, Charles and Victoria, his brothers, John and Charlie, and the mayor Bill Hartsfield at their home on Milledge Avenue, Atlanta, Ga. in 1913

of his fabulous career in the business Coca-Cola, William Hartsfield himself was moving ahead in a different field." [2] He had his eye on a political career.

the first airplane he had ever seen

By 1909, Bill, as he was now called, had began his love affair with the city of Atlanta. He went to Candler field near Hapeville, Ga., (also known as Candler Racetrack) one late afternoon to watch the racing. It was there he saw the first airplane he had ever seen. It was a monoplane flown by a Frenchman named Moisant. "It was the first of thousands of planes that in years to come would land and take off at a place that was first to be known as Candler Field, later as Atlanta Municipal Airport, and finally as Hartsfield International." [3]

Courtesy of Monty Cheshire, grandson of W. B. Hartsfield. William B. Hartsfield and Pearl Williams Hartsfield

In 1913, Bill was prospering and asked Pearl Williams to be his bride. Miss Williams, an operator for the Western Union Telegraph Company, was four years older than Hartsfield. She was a gentle, shy person lacking Hartsfield's bounce and vigor, and unable to understand his fierce urge to make a name for himself. Their courtship was sometimes stormy, but their marriage lasted over 47 years.

In 1916, Hartsfield went to work as a law clerk. He also began reading and learning the law at the prestigious legal firm of Rosser, Slaton, Phillips, and Hopkins. Luther Rosser was a legendary figure in and about Georgia legal circles. John Slaton was a one-time Georgia governor who gained national attention for his courage when he commuted the death sentence of Leo Frank in 1915 (a famous case about the murder of Mary Phagan, later made into a movie). Being associated with men of this caliber, taught Hartsfield that if he were to travel in the same sophisticated circles, he would have to learn far more than he had learned in high school and business school.

Now, he had a wife to support and knew that he and Pearl wanted to start a family. Going to college was out of the question. His solution was simple, he would educate himself. Through the years, he often talked about how proud he was of the fact that he was self educated and would often boast that the Atlanta Public Library was his alma mater. He learned humanities and the law. He even wrote to the deans at some prestigious colleges, telling them that he had foolishly dropped out of

2. William Berry Hartsfield, Mayor of Atlanta. By Harold H. Martin. Copyright 1978 by the University of Georgia Press, Athens GA 30602, p.8
3. Ibid. W. B. H., Mayor of Atlanta p. 12

high school. He asked for a list of books to help him learn on his own. The suggestions of books came pouring in, and night after night for a period of several years, he read many books from the public library.

"Hartsfield was pretty close to Slaton," states Harold Sheats, who in his capacity of Fulton County attorney, had extensive dealings with the Mayor. Sheats said, "He was a protégé of Governor Slaton. That helped him. Governor Slaton had the respect of the business community, Fulton Bag and Cotton Mill, and all the insurance companies. He had the money behind him, and of course he was able to help Hartsfield get the support of the upper element of the people in Atlanta." [4]

In 1918 (some accounts say 1917), Hartsfield passed the Georgia Bar. It was not only a proud moment for him, but for his family as well.

In 1917, a tragic event occurred that shaped Bill's life for many years. He and Pearl, who had only been married four years, had recently moved into their home on Boulevard Terrace. Along with their new son, William Berry Jr., they had barely gotten settled in when on the morning of May 21, 1917, the great Atlanta fire broke out. They got out safely with only a few possessions, but their house was burned along with all the others on the street.

After the fire, many Atlanta residents slept in the streets for a while. The Hartsfield's were a little luckier. They moved into his parent's home on Millage Avenue where they were welcomed. They remained in his parent's home for the next twenty-seven years. They probably would have moved on to another house on their own, but the next year Bill's father, Charles Hartsfield, died from a flu epidemic. Bill wanted to help care for his mother, so he continued to live with her.

4.Living Atlanta, An Oral History Of The City, 1914-1948. By Clifford M. Kuhn, Harlon E. Joyce, & E. Bernard West. Copyright 1990 by the University of Georgia Press Athens, GA 30602. Published in conjunction with the Atlanta Historic Society, Atlanta, Georgia 30305.

Courtesy of Monty Cheshire, grandson of W. B. Hartsfield. Hartsfield's mother, Victoria

his mother had the greatest influence on his life

Charles had worked as a skilled tinsmith all of his life. Although he never received a formal education, Bill thought there was a quality about his father somewhat like a philosopher or a teacher. Charles was respected by Bill and his brothers John and Charles Jr. He had always required proper behavior from his sons as they grew up. With the exception of Sundays, he spent most of his life in his work clothes. Charles was sixty-nine years old when he passed away.

It was Bill's mother, Victoria, who had the greatest influence on his life. From his childhood through his married years, he still lived in her home. Bill learned a lot from his mother that shaped his character. Hartsfield learned two major things from his mother. First, the southern cause was well worth being remembered. It's history should be dramatized in tangible forms like the Cyclorama and the Stone Mountain carvings. Secondly, that he should treat all men fairly, regardless if they were white or black, rich or poor, Yankee or Southerner, always understanding of their weaknesses and being tolerant of their faults. It was a lesson that Hartsfield, a man with a quick temper, would often forget in the many fierce political battles that were to come over the course of his life.

Later, Hartsfield wondered how he could tell who would make a good city employee. His mother, in her wisdom, told him to throw a plank with a nail in it into the street. Then watch to see who passed by and who stopped to pick it up. The latter, she said, would be a good employee.

In 1919, Pearl and Bill had their second child, a daughter whom they named Mildred. (Mildred passed away in early 2012. She was the mother of Monty Cheshire, whom I have already stated is the closest living relative of Mayor Hartsfield).

As the 1920's began, Hartsfield was already looking toward a political career, knowing that it would revolve around The City of Atlanta. His love affair with the city had begun years earlier. At every step of his progress, Bill Hartsfield supported Atlanta. In 1921, he opened his own law office. In 1923, he began his political career, successfully running for the first of two three-year terms as an alderman in the City of Atlanta in the Third Ward.

Courtesy of Monty Cheshire, grandson of W. B. Hartsfield, William B. Hartsfield"s Re-election Campaign (circa 1940's)

Chapter 2 - Who's Hartsfield?

Courtesy of Dale Hartsfield. William B. Hartsfield's Re-election Campaign Poster - circa 1940's. Found at garage sale by Dale's sister, Marsha Hartsfield Hendricks in 2008. Dale has it framed and hanging in his home office

Hartsfield as Chairman of the NEW aviation committee

Hartsfield was soon made Chairman of the NEW aviation committee, put together by the city and then Mayor Walter Sims. During his six-year position as a city alderman, Hartsfield worked tirelessly toward the development of the airport. Many have said that Hartsfield did more for the Atlanta airport from its beginning to this day, than any other single individual in the history of what is now the world's busiest airport. The next chapter will deal with the history of the airport.

In 1927, Hartsfield made the acquaintance of John Steinmetz, a young man who was as much addicted to ground transportation by motor vehicle as Hartsfield was to air transportation. John Steinmetz came to Atlanta from Saint Paul, Minnesota, in the mid twenties, with the idea that he could develop a network of motor-coach and truck lines that would put trains and streetcars out of business.

Hartsfield was Steinmetz's lawyer. Over the next several years, Steinmetz, backed by a Midwestern businessman, began buying up several southern bus lines running in all directions out of Atlanta. Hartsfield shared Steinmetz's conviction that busses were cheaper and more efficient carriers than electric streetcars and trackless trolleys. He was so convinced, in fact, that in 1932 and 1933, he and Steinmetz tried to buy the electric streetcar lines in Rome, Georgia,

Anniston, Alabama, and Columbia, South Carolina with the thought of replacing them with bus lines. The power companies would have been happy to sell but were prevented by state laws that would not permit separation of the street railways.

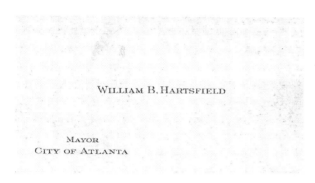

Courtesy of Monty Cheshire, grandson of W. B. Hartsfield.
Hartsfield's first business card as Mayor of Atlanta, 1936

In 1933, Hartsfield returned to politics. He won a state legislature seat from Fulton County. There, he found himself going back to his first love; air travel, airplanes and the promotion of Atlanta as a great regional air terminal. In the House, his first act was to initiate a bill that would authorize a county or a city, or the combination of the two, to build and operate airports whose facilities could be rented to airline operators and concessionaires. Obviously, he was thinking of the Atlanta airport.

Although a representative of Fulton County in the General Assembly, the group that was still closest to his heart was Atlanta. Sometimes, when he felt that his fellow legislators were being unsympathetic to Atlanta's special needs, he would explode in a fit of rage that would bring the reporters running from the pressroom. Thus began his volatile personal style that would be typical of Bill Hartsfield in all of his years in politics. He was one who governed with an iron fist throughout his political career.

the office of mayor

In 1934, he ran for and won the legislative seat again. At the end of this second term in the legislature, he was ready to make his move for the office he really wanted. "In 1936 he ran against the aging James L. Key for the office of mayor." [5]

Mayor Key was a veteran of political wars. Hartsfield was also a veteran politician by now and they both told lies and half truths about each other in an ugly campaign.

Voters in Atlanta seemed unimpressed by what Key and Hartsfield had said about each other. In the primary, they favored Hartsfield slightly: 8,951 votes to 8,534 for Key. A third candidate, businessman James L. Wells, got 3,073 votes. In the runoff, Hartsfield easily won 12,348 to 8,174.

Genuinely moved, he addressed the voters of Atlanta thanking them for their support. His wife, Pearl, and his children Bill Jr. and Mildred shared in his victory. However, Bill's thoughts turned to his mother, Victoria, who had died at the age of eighty-three earlier that year. He told the crowd, "If there

Courtesy of Monty Cheshire, grandson of W. B. Hartsfield.
Hartsfield's Re-election Campaign postcard for his Primary Sept. 7, 1949

were but one thing in the world I could have now, it would be to have my dear mother, who passed away last February, with me. She was always my inspiration and chief supporter in my former races for alderman and member of the legislature. When I take office as mayor, the first thing I am going to

5. Ibid. W.B.H., Mayor of Atlanta p. 18

do is place her picture on my desk, and know I can look there and find the right answer to many of the perplexing problems that are ahead of me." [6]

In December 1936, right before Hartsfield was to take office in January, Robert Woodruff, the president of Coca-Cola, held out a helping hand to the city. The city, like many, was in desperate financial straights in the midst of the depression.

"Woodruff, at Hartsfield's request, let it be known that The Coca-Cola Company would absorb the full amount of the December payroll, some $730,000, going to four thousand city employees, many of whom were school teachers." [7] This was a huge boost for the city as Hartsfield first took the office of Mayor.

On January 4, 1937, Hartsfield addressed the city council in his inaugural address and plainly outlined the problems they faced. The city was thirteen million dollars in debt. With the city nearly bankrupt, Hartsfield noted that this was the city's largest crisis.

Other problems that plagued the city as Hartsfield took the Mayor's office were traffic, a police department that had some dishonest and inefficient members, and the fact that some people were receiving city services at little or no cost. Alcohol license fees were not being regulated and alcohol was sold in places that were not regulated at all. The city was also taking care of many services that both the county and the city were using. These were burdens that Hartsfield would strive to change.

So, with the city almost broke as Hartsfield took the mayor's reigns, his first and most pressing concern was the city's financial condition. He noted that the city had been operating on an out-of-date system of budgeting that allowed it to spend on a basis of expected revenues, a hit or miss plan that at its best created an ever increasing deficit. The word was out in the city financial circles that Robert Woodruff had full confidence in the honesty, character, and financial ability of Bill Hartsfield. The banks were now a little more reassured and willingly helped the new Mayor refinance the most urgent obligations.

The legislature then took the next, and probably the most important, step. At

6. Ibid. W.B.H., Mayor of Atlanta p. 19-20

Courtesy of Coca-Cola Company, Atlanta, GA. Robert Woodruff, long time President of Coca-Cola and life long friend of William B. Hartsfield (circa 1930's)

7. Ibid. W.B.H., Mayor of Atlanta p. 20

Hartsfield's urging, it passed legislation setting up a model financial plan for the city. That legislation stated that no city department could budget more than 99 percent of the previous year's receipts. The city council went even further, usually limiting the budget to only 95 percent to provide a margin of safety over the next few years.

One decision that helped the city's finances and operating budget to work was that the city did not borrow from bonds that had been sold to build expressways, schools, parks, and other capital improvements, as they had done in the past. This helped the bonds to sell at a premium.

Hartsfield pushed for more efficient management by the city department heads. The city department heads eliminated 165 unnecessary positions in Hartsfield's first year in office.

in 1939 the city's budget was in the black

The city was gradually coming out of the depression in 1938. However, more income was needed. Hartsfield declared that Fulton County should assume more of the burden for streets, hospitals and other areas of city services that were shared by the city and the county. He called for higher licensing fees for alcohol sales and for the license laws to be strictly enforced. By 1939, the city's budget was half a million dollars in the black, and its credit rating was high.

Hartsfield had campaigned on cleaning up the police department. He insisted that one thing the people of Atlanta were in complete agreement on was the need to give the department an immediate and complete overhaul. The about face Hartsfield promised came quickly.

Courtesy of Monty Cheshire, grandson of W. B. Hartsfield. Hartsfield often used children in his photos for political campaigns

The city's new police chief, Marion A. Hornsby, was appointed by Hartsfield a few days after his inauguration. He began to make some major differences within the department. Most of the changes were good. Immediately after Hornsby's appointment, the Atlanta Police Department launched a strong movement against gamblers and racketeers, mainly against a lottery operation called the "bug." By early spring, the outraged "bug men" were sending the mayor anonymous threats and Chief Hornsby thought it would be a good idea to give him a bodyguard.

With the police racing through town chasing speeders and/or suspected bug pickup men, some of the law abiding citizens started complaining, claiming their lives were being endangered. These protests resulted in the use of the "hidden police," who would charge out of a side street to overtake a speeder before he knew what happened. This tactic became politically damaging to Hartsfield. Many who were caught speeding charged that the city was actually trying to raise revenue instead of cleaning up some of its problems.

Chapter 2 - Who's Hartsfield?

Courtesy of Monty Cheshire, grandson of W. B. Hartsfield. Photo of Monte, Mayor Hartsfield, his daughter and son-in-law, Mildred and Jimmy Cheshire 1957

the airport remained on his mind

As Hartsfield made changes throughout the city in the late 1930's and early 1940's, the airport remained on his mind. Over the next years, he would continue to strive to improve the airport. He insisted that ways must be found to improve the traffic control tower and lengthen the runways. He knew that this would be a vital part of the growth of the airport and the city.

With the city's finances in good order and its police department reorganized and running efficiently, Hartsfield turned to another idea which he would endorse with great enthusiasm throughout his years as mayor. He sought to develop Atlanta as a great tourist center.

He remembered the stories his mother had told him about the Civil War and the time he spent as a boy prowling through some of the old battlefields.

Hartsfield was convinced that Atlanta's history was one of its cherished resources. He felt that the Cyclorama could draw thousands of visitors to Atlanta every year. Stone Mountain, although not in the city, would easily be made into a famous tourist attraction that would be supported by the Cyclorama and other attractions in the city. His hope was that the federal government would make Stone Mountain into a National Park.

Hartsfield was also determined that "his" city would not only be a place of business and industry, but also a place of beauty. With this in mind, he proposed several quiet little parks be built between the tall buildings. In 1940, the Joel Hurt Park became the first of many that he proposed. While beautifying the inner city, Hartsfield worked tirelessly throughout his long career to push the city limits further and further outward. He worked toward annexing Buckhead, among other areas, into the city.

the great novel
Gone with the Wind

In the spring of 1936, Margaret Mitchell, an Atlanta native, wrote and published her great novel, **Gone with the Wind**. The movie rights were bought by David Selznick. Over the next few years, rumors circulated about the movie premiere being in Atlanta. These rumors were not supported by the film industry. Mayor Hartsfield knew that this would mean a lot to Atlanta. He worked toward making the rumors a reality. There was reason to suspect that the Mayor had started the rumors in the first place.

There were other rumors that the film would premiere in New York. Hartsfield said this was the worst outrage since Sherman burned Atlanta. Hartsfield and the city waited apprehensively. Finally, on November 4th 1939, Howard Dietz of MGM sent a telegram stating that the **Gone With the Wind** premiere would be at the Lowe's Grand Theater in Atlanta, on Friday, December 15, 1939.

Courtesy of Monty Cheshire, grandson of W. B. Hartsfield. William B. Hartsfield's photo with Bob Hope at the Atlanta Fox Theatre (circa 1940's)

Courtesy of Monty Cheshire, grandson of W. B. Hartsfield. "Official U. S. Navy Photograph" Mayor Hartsfield, Margaret Mitchell and Navy officers aboard one of the USS Atlanta Cruisers, December 3, 1944

Hartsfield was probably the film's most valuable promoter. He notified **Life Magazine** among other forms of media, urging them to cover the grand event. He sent thousands of invitations to the mayors and other dignitaries of all the southern states.

The premiere was a great success, with a great ball where the crowd danced to waltzes and thousands lined the streets and cheered. Actor Clark Gable and actresses Vivian Leigh and Carole Lombard (Gable's wife) attended the festivities.

Willard Cope of the **Atlanta Constitution** summed it up this way, "It was Hollywood, but it was also Atlanta. It was theater, but it was also life."[8] It was also Hartsfield! He had a way of making this kind of excitement thrilling for the City of Atlanta and its people, who he always seemed to put in the spotlight.

The premiere was a proud victory for Hartsfield. Maybe too proud! As the 1940 election approached, he was extremely confident. Therefore, he did not campaign with the same fervor that he had in the past. He had gotten the city into the black in less than four years, cleaned up the police force from its problems and brought worldwide attention to Atlanta with the **Gone With the Wind** premiere.

8. Ibid. W.B.H., Mayor of Atlanta p. 31

Photo on right: Courtesy of Monty Cheshire, grandson of W. B. Hartsfield. Clark Gable, Carole Lombard, Gable's wife, with W. B. Hartsfield and Mildred Hartsfield, Hartsfield's daughter, at the premiere of Gone With The Wind at the Loew's Grand Theatre in Atlanta on December 15, 1939

Courtesy of Joy Hartsfield, great neice of W. B. Hartsfield. Election campaign celebration. (circa 1940's)

However, his political luck had run out.

The Mayors election on September 4th, 1940, was one of the closest races ever held in Atlanta. The issue of the "hiding police," along with the fact that Hartsfield did not campaign with the fervor of his first election, cost him. He lost to the former Chamber of Commerce president, Roy LeCraw. LeCraw promised to do away with the hiding police if elected. He also charged that taxes had been raised on the honest working citizens of Atlanta, but that thousands in the city did not pay taxes. Hartsfield lost by 83 votes, 11,410 to 11,327.

Hartsfield contested the election, but nothing came of it. However, his absence from City Hall would be brief. In the spring of 1942, Mayor LeCraw, angered by the Japanese attack on Pearl Harbor, resigned in order to go into the U. S Army. In May of 1942, a special election was held and Hartsfield easily won over eight other candidates. For the next twenty years, the office would be his.

Hartsfield was the longest serving mayor in the City of Atlanta. He was the city's chief executive from 1937 until he retired in 1961, except for a limited wartime period. When he retired from the office of Mayor in 1961, the city had doubled in population to nearly a half a million people and had tripled in land area. He was serious about keeping the city clean and honest. During his time in office, the city grew bigger, busier, and more beautiful with each passing year. Atlanta was such a part of him that he could not separate it from his personal life. He was of one mind and one spirit with the city.

Hartsfield faced many issues as he took office the first and the second time. The first time, the city, as was the country, was fighting its way out of the Depression. In 1942, when he took office the second time, we were in the middle of WWII.

One problem that faced Hartsfield, the city, and even the country was race relations. Hartsfield, like most whites, did not want the blacks to vote, or hold any type of office early in his career.

In 1926, he had even introduced an ordinance barring black barbers from cutting the hair of a white man. In the 1936 mayoral campaign, Governor Eugene Talmadge and his opponent James L. Key, both called him a segregationist. However, as time moved forward, Hartsfield began to soften his stance on the black population.

By the mid 1940's, it was becoming clear that the black man could no longer be held down simply because of his skin color. Sure, race problems continue even today. But in the south, the forties would become the decade when things began to change. Many black soldiers served our country well during World War II.

As mayor, Hartsfield's racial changes were small at first. Instead of removing signs at rest rooms and restaurants that said "white" and "colored," he first just reduced them in size, until they could hardly be seen at all. Finally, they were gone.

It was a slow, tactful transition that helped Hartsfield become "The Mayor of all the People." This would become not only a proud boast of his, but also a campaign. He kept the ever increasing black vote throughout his career.

Also in the forties, Hartsfield began requiring city clerks, when sending correspondence to black citizens, to address them as Mr., Mrs., or Miss. This caused a lot of complaining at City Hall when he gave this order.

This change, possibly, began with the memory of his mother who had once told him that the responsibility of the man in public office was to help people who were trying to better themselves. With black soldiers enlisted in WWII, this became very evident.

Courtesy of Joy Hartsfield

Hartsfield strived not to allow blacks to be put down or kept from opportunities in education, economics and eventually even in politics. With the KKK acting violently against blacks at times, Hartsfield, as mayor, vowed that Atlanta would move forward without violence.

In 1944, he came up with a slogan that would follow the city well into the Ivan Allen years as mayor. That slogan was, "Atlanta, a City too busy to Hate." The slogan was genius! It seemed that all of Atlanta and the nation outside of the south embraced it. Racial attitudes and problems had begun to change, especially in Atlanta. Of course, racial problems were not solved. But for a southern city, Atlanta was very progressive in its thinking.

In 1948, for the first time, Hartsfield appointed eight black policemen to the city's force. He had purged the force from active Klansman and along with a very capable police chief, Herbert Jenkins, they made the appointments after carefully selecting the eight.

From the blacks standpoint this would become a major breakthrough in race relations in the city.

Hartsfield never failed to praise the City of Atlanta

No matter the event or forum, Hartsfield never failed to praise the City of Atlanta. But, like most politicians, Hartsfield had his share of enemies. He was a powerful man and often rubbed people the wrong way. Despite problems along the way, no one ever questioned his commitment to doing what was right for the City of Atlanta.

Hartsfield, a devout Baptist, was held in high esteem not only by the black population but also by the Atlanta Catholic and Jewish communities.

Because he was ever in the limelight, he often had publicity pictures taken of him at all kinds of events. One picture that caused him to beam with pride was one of his 3 ½ month-old grandson, Monty. Hartsfield's daughter, Mildred, had brought Monty to the mayor's office. Monty clutched the mayor's tie with one hand and his gavel with the other. Hartsfield knew the value of using the baby kissing technique in politics. He often used Monty as a political prop.

In 2009 Monty told me, "Since birth, I had been transported back and forth to Atlanta to visit my grandparents, my mother's parents, Paw Paw and Mummy. Both spent lots of time over me, documented by memories and by 16 mm home movies shot by my dad and Paw Paw before the times I can remember. I always enjoyed those visits and he was always The Mayor, apparently an important man because of all the phone calls, his raised voice into the receiver and his muttering afterward. You wouldn't want him mad at you or worse, disappointed in you." [9]

9. Email quote from Monty Cheshire, 2009

Hartsfield mastered his handling of the press throughout his career. Most reporters liked him, often because of his volatile streak. It seemed to always give them a story. Sometimes it even got him into trouble. He was a confidant man, but was often troubled not so much at his personal life but at the constant matters that affected the City of Atlanta. As the city grew, so did the problems. But his success in guiding the city through the war

Courtesy of Monty Chesire, Grandson of Mayor Hartsfield. Monty's picture taken with Mayor in 1947

and the years thereafter made his name known in Washington and nationally. He was called on many times because of his influence in causes around the country.

On December 7th, 1946, an Atlanta tragedy took place. Early in the morning, 119 persons died in the Winecoff Hotel fire. Many of them were young girls and boys in town for a YMCA meeting. It was the world's worst hotel fire at the time.

Photo on left: Courtesy of Monty Cheshire, grandson of W. B. Hartsfield. William B. Hartsfield's photo with Walt Disney in California (circa 1940's)

Hartsfield, deeply distressed, moved quickly to lay down rules for remodeling and construction on high rise buildings to hopefully keep such tragedies from occurring in the future.

By the time the 100th anniversary of the city was being organized in 1948, the city was experiencing real growth. The city was now the 28th largest in the nation with some 350,000 living within the city and 595,000 more in the metro area. With his showman's abilities, Hartsfield certainly didn't let this pass without some hoopla. Margaret Mitchell came to city hall, and cut the city's birthday cake and gave the first slice to Hartsfield. Hartsfield touted the accomplishments of the city and predicted that the real growth had just begun.

The year also marked the 25th anniversary of his true friend and supporter, Robert Woodruff, at the helm of Coca-Cola. Under Woodruff's leadership, the company had helped put Atlanta on the map. Atlanta, after all, was also the birthplace of Coke.

Early in 1949, Hartsfield thought of leaving the mayor's office. His name had been mentioned as a possible candidate for the newly formed office of Assistant Secretary of Commerce for Aeronautics. This job was to be the "boss" of Civil Aviation in America.

In March, he spent a couple of days thinking about it while recovering from a severe sinus infection in the hospital. But, he decided to run for Mayor of Atlanta once again when he heard in early May that the job would not be filled for a while.

Courtesy of Monty Cheshire, grandson of W. B. Hartsfield. William B. Hartsfield last photo as the Mayor of Atlanta with the Atlanta skyline in 1961

Courtesy of Monty Cheshire, grandson of W. B. Hartsfield. Mayor William B. Hartsfield's with candidate John F. Kennedy taken at Warm Springs, GA

The 1950's brought more good news for Hartsfield and Atlanta. The airport was continuing to grow and doing well! The city was doing fine in most all areas. Race relations were in good health. Hartsfield's handling of the NAACP annual convention in Atlanta in 1951 brought praise from the **Atlanta Constitution**. The expressway system was on track in Atlanta and throughout the country.

1951 was a landmark year for Hartsfield! That was the year that the city annexed Buckhead and Cascade Heights into the city limits. Actually, it was not called an annexation, but a "Plan of Improvement." A local government commission had been studying the improvement and the Georgia Legislature voted it into law in 1951 with it taking effect January 1, 1952. This improvement eliminated costly duplication of county and city services. To Hartsfield's delight, it more than tripled the land area of the city to 118 square miles and added some one hundred thousand citizens.

making him the mayor's mayor

In 1952, as anticipated, Hartsfield was elected the president of the American Municipal Association, making him the mayors' mayor. His election to this national office, coupled with the fact that he should easily win the 1953 election, prompted Ralph

McGill, the editor in chief of **The Atlanta Constitution**, to suggest to his old friend Ben Hibbs of the **Saturday Evening Post**, that he write an article about Hartsfield for the **Saturday Evening Post**.

In the article, McGill wrote of Hartsfield's accomplishments and how he had served the city for over 15 years without a hint of corruption. The article also had some criticism of Hartsfield: mainly that he was a difficult man to support because he had a habit of arguing with people instead of giving them the old political pat on the back! The article tentatively was to be called "Mayor of a Showcase City." The title fit. However, the actual title ended up being "You'd Think He Owns Atlanta." That was a quote from Robert Snodgrass, the president of the Atlanta Chamber of Commerce. [10]

In 1953, Hartsfield beat Charlie Brown in the mayor's race, again. And he did own the city figuratively for four more years. A name that many Atlantans will remember is Helen Bullard. She helped Hartsfield through the 1940's and the 1950's as a member of his staff with many issues including race relations. This helped him get elected again in 1953.

10. Ibid. W.B.H., Mayor of Atlanta p. 99

Courtesy of Monty Cheshire, grandson of W. B. Hartsfield. Hartsfield with General Dwight D. Eisenhower in an Atlanta parade, September 1952

Courtesy of Monty Cheshire, grandson of W. B. Hartsfield. On the set in California of "Never So Few" in 1959. (Left to right) Monty Cheshire, Frank Sinatra, Jesse Draper (Chairman, Atlanta Aviation Committee), Mayor Hartsfield, couple (California cousins of Jimmy Cheshire) and Jimmy Cheshire

Hartsfield did have some problems with the Negro Voters League concerning the fact that there were no black firemen in the city at the time. Ms. Bullard had gone to Grace Hamilton, a highly respected black leader, and asked for her advice on how to get around the problem. Hartsfield listened to what Hamilton had said and he won the black vote again.

In 1957, although he won again, Lester Maddox had won the majority of the white vote. Many rural Georgians had been moving to Atlanta throughout the 1950's. A lot of them did not share Hartsfield's ideas on race and moving the city forward with the now famous slogan, "A City too busy to Hate."

Monty, his now 10 year old grandson, helped with Hartsfield's 1957 election. He also continued an informal policy that he had in his elections since 1936. He would go out into the streets and ask citizens what they would do about a particular problem if they were in his place. It was a crude, but sometimes effective, method of polling. He would think about their answers and based on them, decide what to do that is, if it generally agreed with his own ideas.

In November of 1957, **Fortune Magazine** named Hartsfield one of the nation's nine best mayors.

Hartsfield was outraged at the bombing of the Jewish Temple in Atlanta in 1958. His anger brought him national recognition and showed once again that famous slogan that we were a city too busy to hate. In the late 1950's, people were moving to Atlanta from all parts of the U.S. and around the world. The city continued to grow. [11]

In 1959, the city built a half-million-dollar primate house at the Grant Park Zoo. One of the early inhabitants was a baby gorilla that the zoo attendants named Willie B. The zoo became a national attraction. Hartsfield, with his PR talent ever present, told Atlantans who had grumbled over the city paying so much for the building, that Willie B's appeal would help bring people to visit the zoo. He was right! Willie B. was one of Atlanta's most famous attractions. Willie B. brought thousands to Grant Park over the next 39 years before dying in February 2000.

Among some of Hartsfield's other accomplishments, were the ever expanding aviation facilities (see next chapter), the development of the Chattahoochee River, operating the city on a cash basis for most of his long career as Mayor, and construction of Grady Hospital and Buford Dam.

11. Ibid. W.B.H., Mayor of Atlanta p. 132-133

Courtesy of Ray Leader, Federal Aviation Administration-Retired, Hartsfield-Jackson Atlanta International Airport. Atlanta Airport (circa 1960's)

Courtesy of Dale Hartsfield. Willie B, named after W. B. Hartsfield, at the Atlanta Zoo

Willie B.
1958 - 2000

"And in setting him free, perhaps we set ourselves free to help us learn that we can live together in peace with all of the animals that God has created."

Although not in the city, the dam site and the lake constructed by the Corps of Engineers would be, Hartsfield argued, a benefit not only to the city but to the whole area, giving us adequate water supplies for years to come.

Then, things began to change for Hartsfield. He wanted to run again in 1961, but he also knew that he was now in his 70's. He was in love with a younger lady and had asked Pearl for a divorce. He knew he could not get a divorce and win the election. On June 7, 1961, he announced that he would not be running for Mayor in the fall election.

Hartsfield filed for divorce from Pearl on November 3, 1961. The divorce was granted February 9, 1962. Hartsfield's daughter, Mildred Cheshire, sided with her mother, wanting to make sure her needs were taken care of.

On July 11, 1962, he married Tollie B. Tolan of Athens Georgia, in a surprise ceremony at the home of Dr. and Mrs. Thomas J. Harold of Winterville, Georgia. Hartsfield had known Tollie for nearly 12 years. At 72, he was 32 years older than her when they married. They lived very happily for nearly 8 years. In fact, he once said they were the happiest of his life. However, he went against the advice of his closest friend and most valued consultant, Robert Woodruff, in his decision to divorce Pearl and marry Tollie.

On January 2, 1962, Hartsfield said he was proud to turn over the city to his successor, Ivan Allen, a city that was strong and healthy. 1961 bills were all paid and the city had a cash excess of over 3 million dollars, the largest in city history.

In his retirement years from the City of Atlanta, Hartsfield worked as a consultant for the Ford Foundation and Coca-Cola. He also was elected the President of The Southeastern Fair located at Lakewood Park Fairgrounds in south Atlanta.

Hartsfield continued his involvement in city, civic, and cultural events during the 1960's and early 1970's.

Just before Christmas, 1970, Hartsfield's heart began to fail. His heart actually stopped beating at Saint Joseph's Hospital, but the staff there was able to bring him back. He did seem to get better over the next couple of months, but he passed away just before midnight on the evening of February 22, 1971, a week before his eighty-first birthday.

After his death, **Time Magazine** wrote he had "influenced the city's development more than any person in modern times." [12]

what others said of Hartsfield

In 2009, I interviewed former Atlanta Mayor Sam Massell in his Buckhead office, asking him to tell me about Hartsfield. (Sam Massell was a one-term mayor of Atlanta, but has held the unofficial title as the "Mayor of Buckhead" for years.) Massell said of Hartsfield, "Hartsfield was smart, known for his integrity and he was an honest man." Massell also said, "I was fond of Bill. He was a shrewd politician." Laughing, he said, "He was known for parking anywhere he wanted to park." Massell was the mayor of Atlanta when Hartsfield died. Massell and his administration named the airport for Hartsfield shortly after his death in 1971.

Massell, who is Jewish, told me about prejudices in Atlanta. He said that Hartsfield recognized the

12. Ibid. W.B.H., Mayor of Atlanta p. 210 (Time Magazine 3-8-71)

Courtesy of Monty Cheshire, grandson of W. B. Hartsfield. Mayor W. B. Hartsfield and cast of bust placed in Atlanta City Hall

TERMS AND CONDITIONS

ALL EXPENSE RATE: $1,350.00

1. **AIR TRANSPORTATION** (Tourist) on Pan American World Airlines.
2. **RAIL** transportation abroad, with reserved seats and bed in double compartment for night travel.
3. **ACCOMMODATIONS:** First Class Hotels in Middle East and Europe, basis two in a room, with private bath where available.
4. **FOOD:** Three meals daily, including continental breakfast table d'hote lunch and dinner. Meals on train and plane while enroute.
5. **SIGHTSEEING AND EXCURSIONS:** as outlined in the itinerary, with English-speaking guides.
6. **TRANSFERS:** Passengers and baggage from railroad stations and city air terminals to hotels and vice versa.
7. **TAXES AND TIPS** at hotels, to drivers, guides, porters and interpreters.
8. **TOUR CONDUCTOR** service.
9. **ORIENTATION FEATURES:** Meetings and receptions with leaders in host nations.

NOT INCLUDED: Cost of U.S. passport, personal items such as laundry and beverages, etc.

RESPONSIBILITY. A. T. HENDERSON CO., INC., N. Y., and/or its agents act only as agent for the passenger and assumes no responsibility nor liability in connection with the services of transportation companies and individuals furnishing services for which tickets and coupons are issued, neither will they be responsible nor liable for any personal injury, delay, accident or loss of personal property, or for additional expense caused by circumstances beyond their control. Additional expense if any shall be borne by the passengers; conversely refund will be made to the passenger if any savings is effected thereby.

Any and/or all transportation companies herein mentioned shall have or incur no responsibility or liability to any traveler, aside from their liability as common carriers. The airlines concerned are not to be held responsible for any act, omission, or event, during the time passengers are not on board their planes or conveyance. The passage contract in use by the airlines concerned, when issued, shall constitute the sole contract between the airlines and the purchaser of these tours and/or passenger.

All rates shown in this program are based upon current tariffs, taxes and rates of exchange and are subject to adjustment in the event of changes therein, prior to tour departure. Baggage is "at owner's risk" throughout the journey; liability of carriers for baggage and other property of passengers is limited to their liability as common carriers; insurance may be arranged at time of booking. Small articles (coats, wraps, umbrellas, etc.) are entirely under care of passengers, who are cautioned against the risk attached to their being left in conveyances while sightseeing.

TRAVELWISE, operated by Harry F. Brown, Director of WORLDWAYS, Educational Tour Division of A. T. Henderson Co., Inc., long experienced and specialists in MIDDLE EAST TRAVEL.

41 EAST 42nd STREET
New York 17, N. Y.

U.S. MAYORS
ON AN
EXCITING ADVENTURE
THROUGH
THE MIDDLE EAST
AND
THE HOLY LAND
WITH

17 DAYS

ALL-INCLUSIVE

$1350.

HON. WILLIAM B. HARTSFIELD
PRES. AMERICAN MUNICIPAL ASSOCIATION
and
MAYOR OF ATLANTA, GEORGIA

LEAVING N. Y. — OCT. 18, 1953
RETURNING N. Y. — NOV. 3, 1953

PAN AMERICAN WORLD AIRWAYS

Brochure - Front & Back Cover - Mayor's Travel Itinerary October 18, 1953 thru November 3, 1953

THE U. S. MAYOR'S STUDY TOUR has been designed to give a firsthand vivid picture of life and problems in the Middle East.

The MAYORS will..............................

SEE ACROPOLIS in ATHENS . . . BOSPORUS in TURKEY . . . Baalbek in LEBANON . . . Philadelphian Amphitheatre in AMMAN . . . Church of Nativity in BETHLEHEM . . . Church of the Holy Sepulchre . . . Dome of the Rock (Mosque of Omar in Temple area) . . . in the Old City of Jerusalem . . . ISRAEL . . . in the New City of JERUSALEM; BEERSHEBA, TEL AVIV, HAIFA, and Mt. Carmel, Tiberia, Sea of Galilee . . . ROME — Colosseum, Pantheon, St. Peters, the Catacombs . . . PARIS — Modern and Historic Sections.

STUDY a vital underdeveloped area . . . Get factual data about the social, religious, political and economic problems. Learn what our government through E.C.A. and T.C.A. is doing in the area. What each nation visited is doing to bring a fuller life to its people . . . U.N. Technical Assistance, Relief and Works Agency Projects.

MEET U. S. government officials, U. N. personnel, and local Mayors, government, cultural and religious leaders in each country.

JOIN MAYOR HARTSFIELD and SPENCER D. IRWIN, ASSOCIATE EDITOR of the CLEVELAND PLAIN DEALER, who will accompany the Mayors as Foreign Affairs Expert and Associate Tour leader.

Spencer D. Irwin

JOIN TODAY

Early booking is necessary to secure passport and visas, as well as acceptance to the tour.

STUDY TOUR ITINERARY

Oct.			
Sun. 18	IDLEWILD TO PARIS	PA 062 Dep. 1:00 P.M.	
Mon. 19	PARIS	Arr. PARIS 9:45 A.M.	
Tues. 20	PARIS TO ATHENS	AF 470 Dep. 1:40 P.M.	
		Arr. Athens 9:25 P.M.	
Wed. 21	ATHENS TO ISTANBUL	BE 130 Dep. 7:35 P.M.	
		Arr. ISTANBUL 9:25 P.M.	
Thur. 22	ISTANBUL		
Fri. 23	ISTANBUL	Dep. 8:05 A.M.	
	ANKARA	Arr. 9:30 A.M. on DHY 2	
Sat. 24	BEIRUT	Dep. ANKARA 10 A.M.	
		Arr. BEIRUT 1:00 P.M.	
Sun. 25 through	SYRIA, JORDAN and ISRAEL . . . BY Pullman Motorcoach to Baalbek . . . Damascus . . . AMMAN . . . Bethlehem . . . Jerusalem, old and new City . . . then tour through Israel		
Nov.			
Sun. 1	TEL AVIV TO ROME	Dep. LAI #434 at 1:00 A.M.	
1	ROME	Arr. 8:10 A.M.	
Mon. 2	ROME TO NEW YORK	PA 063. Dep. 7:00 P.M.	
Tues. 3	NEW YORK	Arr. IDLEWILD 1:25 P.M.	

Brochure - Inside Pages - Mayor's Travel Itinerary October 18, 1953 thru November 3, 1953

Courtesy of Ray Leader, Federal Aviation Administration (Retired), Hartsfield-Jackson Atlanta International Airport. Atlanta Airport (circa 1960's)

attitudes of prejudices in the city. He knew that he could not change things overnight. He knew that as the mayor, he had to work with the black community. In the 1940's and 1950's, Hartsfield recognized their sophistication and courted the black leadership. He knew the importance of cooperation and he was good at it. Massell also said that Hartsfield worked closely with the large Atlanta Jewish community.

Hartsfield and Massell had some differences in the annexation of Buckhead. Hartsfield said publicly that he needed Buckhead because he needed more white people in the city. Mayor Massell said after Hartsfield's death, "Atlanta will miss Hartsfield forever. He is irreplaceable."

I also spoke with Dick Yarbrough, a retired vice president from BellSouth, a managing director of the 1996 Centennial Olympic Games and currently, a syndicated columnist whose column appears frequently in many Georgia newspapers. Yarbrough said of Mayor Hartsfield, "He governed in a time when there was a 'benevolent dictatorship' in Atlanta, made up of bankers, utility executives and the wealthy, though segregated, blacks. Mayor Hartsfield was a skilled politician and considered 'liberal' for his time. He was also a visionary and recognized the future potential of airline travel before most of us. He was the right man at the right time. The only other mayor that I can compare to him favorably is Ivan Allen. He kept a lid on Atlanta during the Civil Rights demonstrations and kept the city from blowing apart. Another right man at the right time."

In 2012, I spoke with Joy Hartsfield, who along with

her dad, Charlie, stood with me in 2003 during the airport name change. Charlie is the grand nephew of William B. Hartsfield. His grandfather was the mayor's brother. Joy was 12 years old when Mayor Hartsfield died.

She was sick a lot as a child and the Mayor spent a lot of time with her. He would bring her puzzle books and tell her she needed to work on her "Brain Power." When she broke her collarbone, "Uncle Willie" (as she called him) taught her to write with her left hand thereby making her ambidextrous, like the Mayor.

The Mayor also told her to "work at what you are good at" and "you have to work for what you want."

Joy still has the last pocket change that the Mayor had, along with other memorabilia like several of his tie tacks. She also told me that "Uncle Willie often carried an arsenal of guns in his trunk."

Courtesy of the Atlanta Hartsfield-Jackson International Airport. The airport had its own fleet of yellow fire trucks used solely at the Hartsfield Atlanta International Airport from 1971 thru 2003

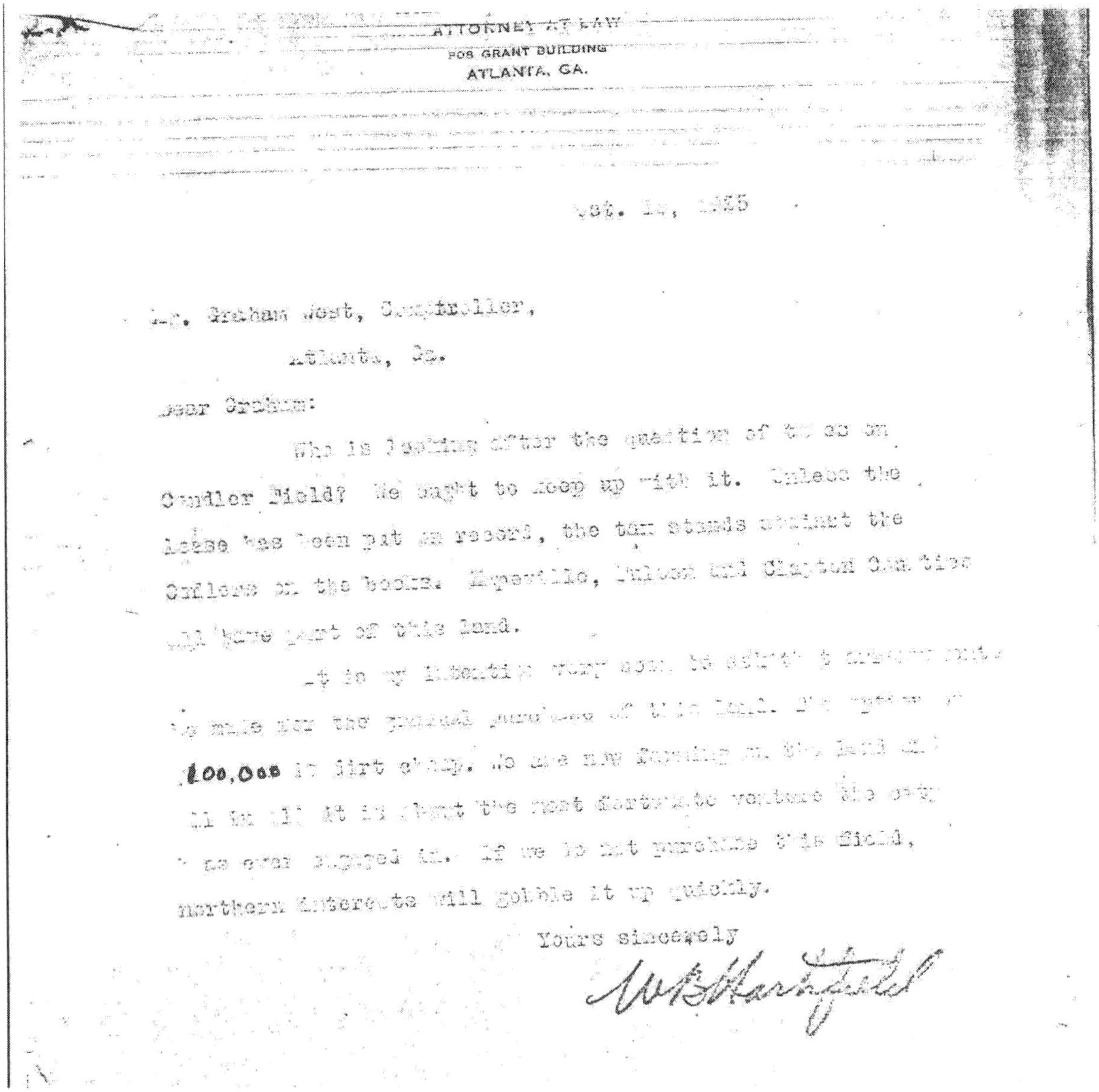

ATTORNEY AT LAW
705 GRANT BUILDING
ATLANTA, GA.

Oct. 14, 1925

Mr. Graham West, Comptroller,
    Atlanta, Ga.

Dear Graham:

Who is looking after the question of taxes on Candler Field? We ought to keep up with it. Unless the lease has been put on record, the tax stands against the Candlers on the books. Hapeville, Fulton and Clayton Counties all have part of this land.

It is my intention very soon to advise a bond issue to make out the actual purchase of this land. The option of $100,000 is dirt cheap. As are now farming it, the land at 11 to all it is about the most daring to venture the city has ever engaged in. If we do not purchase this field, northern interests will gobble it up quickly.

Yours sincerely
W. B. Hartsfield

Courtesy of George Berry, former General Manager of the Atlanta Airport. George Berry found this letter in an old file at City Hall in Atlanta, written by W. B. Hartsfield

WILLIAM BERRY HARTSFIELD
ATTORNEY AT LAW
508 GRANT BUILDING
ATLANTA, GA.

October 15, 1925

Mr. Graham West, Comptroller,
Atlanta, Ga.

Dear Mr. Graham:

Who is looking after the question of taxes on Candler Field? We ought to keep up with it. Unless the lease has been put on record, the tax stands against the Candlers on the books. Hapeville, Fulton and Clayton Counties all have part of this land.

It is my intention very soon to ask that arrangements be made for the gradual purchase of this land. The option of $100,000 is dirt cheap. We are now farming on the land and all in all it is about the most fortunate venture the city has ever engaged in. If we do not purchase this field, northern interests will gobble it up quickly.

Yours sincerely,

(Signed by W.B. Hartsfield)

Duplicated copy of the 1925 letter signed by W. B. Hartsfield

Courtesy of the Atlanta Hartsfield-Jackson International Airport. Candler Racetrack (circa 1920's)

Courtesy of Ray Leader, Federal Aviation Administration (Retired), Hartsfield-Jackson Atlanta International Airport. Atlanta Airport 1927

Chapter Three
The History of an Airport

In less than ninety years, the Atlanta airport progressed from very humble beginnings to becoming the world's busiest airport. After five official name changes, it is currently known as the Hartsfield-Jackson Atlanta International Airport.

The history of this great airport began in 1925. Mayor James L. Key began moving toward air services in 1922. He negotiated a lease for a landing field at a farm off Brown's Mill Road, known as the Nichols estate in southeast Atlanta. The lease was three hundred dollars per month with an option to buy the entire farm for $75,000. However, as Mayor Walter Sims took over in 1923, he was convinced that a better place could be found for less money.

In summing up his accomplishments, Mayor Key prophesied that aviation would grow, but he also acknowledged that Atlanta had many shortcomings regarding air services. Up to that point, the city had been very hesitant to get into the "airport business."

what is an airport

Courtesy of the Atlanta Hartsfield-Jackson International Airport. Eastern & Delta Ticketing 1948

Courtesy of the Atlanta Hartsfield-Jackson International Airport. This building in the background is the 1946 terminal with the observation deck which was Hartsfield's idea. Each person was charged ten cents to go out on the deck

In 1923, Mayor Sims asked a young city alderman, William B. Hartsfield, to check into possibilities about where the city could build an airport. In 1923, most people were still asking, "What is an airport?" Hartsfield on the other hand was already in love with the thought of flying, and wanted Atlanta to have a first-class airport. In 1909, Hartsfield had seen his first plane at Candler racetrack flown by a Frenchman named Moisant. After this encounter, his enthusiasm for flight lasted throughout his life. The Atlanta airport would eventually be built at the old Candler racetrack.

During World War I, from 1914 through the early 1920's, Candler racetrack was used as a landing field for military and private planes. The City of Atlanta had not approved Candler racetrack as a location for an airport, but at that time, it was the only field available for landing planes in the area.

After WWI, two pilots, Beeler Blevins and Doug Davis, began flying people around the Atlanta area for sight-seeing adventures at five dollars a head from the Candler racetrack. In the early 1920's, they began flying Alderman Hartsfield on special missions looking for suitable land for the proposed airport. Later, Hartsfield credited these two pilots for their knowledge in searching for what would make a satisfactory and fitting airfield, including knowing what to avoid.

George Shealey, another WWI pilot, flew Hartsfield over the Atlanta and surrounding areas searching for open land around the city that could possibly be used for an airfield. Hartsfield even took over the controls on one occasion so he could see the terrain from a pilot's eyes. He never piloted another plane after that one flight.

During 1924, Mayor Sims had several meetings with interested aviation supporters. One such meeting was with Lt. Colonel Charles H. Danforth, commander of the Fourth Corps Army Area Air Service. He was searching for suitable airfields in a proposed national network of army airfields.

Colonel Danforth was also working with the United States Post Office who were partnering with the War Department in setting up future air mail routes. The post office was already using air transportation to shuttle the mail. It was quickly becoming a new way of transporting mail around the world.

Colonel Danforth had considerable influence in the search for an airfield near Atlanta. Danforth met with Fulton County commissioners pointing out that if an airfield could not be provided soon, Atlanta may not get an anticipated air mail route and the Army Air Corps would be looking elsewhere. The Fulton County commissioners appointed their own

Courtesy of Ray Leader, Federal Aviation Administration (Retired), Hartsfield-Jackson Atlanta International Airport. Candler Field, Atlanta Airport, January 31, 1928

Chapter 3 - The History of the Airport

committee and requested that the city take action soon.

On September 15, 1924, the City of Atlanta appointed their own committee to work with the county and the Colonel to secure an airfield and arrange appropriations to cover the costs.

County committee members and Colonel Danforth inspected some twenty sites and approved five. On September 17th, **The Atlanta Constitution** reported another site had been approved earlier. It was the 208 acre Nichols estate that had been previously rejected by Mayor Sims because of the cost. The estate was now offered at $65,000.

Courtesy of Coca-Cola. Asa Candler who was a former Atlanta Mayor and the man who really began Coca-Cola, sold his Candler racetrack property to the City of Atlanta for the airport in 1929

what airfield would ever need more than 200 acres

The Nichols estate almost became the airport. It was the only one of many sites inspected by Fulton County and Atlanta committees that met with Colonel Danforth's approval. It had excellent rail access and was more than twice the 100 acre minimum required by the Army Air Corps. After all, "What airfield would ever need more than 200 acres?" [1] Today, Hartsfield-Jackson has approximately 4,700 acres! [2]

In December of 1924, Atlanta Alderman C. D. Knight, announced that Asa G. Candler, Jr., of Coca Cola fame, had offered his family's defunct racetrack in Hapeville to the city rent free for two years, if the city would agree to pay the taxes.

At the December 15th Alderman meeting, officials failed by one vote to overturn Mayor Sims veto of the appropriations on the Nichols estate. The Nichols property was withdrawn on January 1, 1925. The property later became Brown's Mill Park. The loss of that property proved beneficial for Atlanta's airport search.

Asa Candler worked closely with the City of Atlanta about the possibility of using his property as Atlanta's first airport. Candler also wanted the city to buy the property outright at the end of the lease if a price could be agreed upon.

Alderman Hartsfield had looked at the Candler property as well as many others both from the air and the ground. Fellow government officials had financial interests in some of the other properties and put pressure on Hartsfield to look at their land. (Politics have not changed!) However, nothing

1. A Dream Takes Flight, Hartsfield Atlanta International Airport and Aviation in Atlanta. p 18. By Betsy Braden and Paul Hagan. Copyright 1989 by the University of Georgia Press, Athens, GA 30602. Published in conjuction with The Atlanta Historical Society, Atlanta, GA 30305.
2. www.Atlanta-Airport.com (ATL Official website)

Courtesy of Tom Dorsett who is a retired aviator with several private corporations. I met Tom while teaching a class about the Atlanta airport at Kennesaw State Continuing Education in 2012. Photo was A King Air photo taken at the Atlanta Municipal Airport. January 25, 1947

looked more suitable than the Candler land. Alderman Hartsfield recommended that the city lease the land with the 5 year option to buy. On April 16, 1925, Mayor Sims, representing the City of Atlanta, signed a rent-free lease agreement with Charles Howard Candler, acting on behalf of Asa G. Candler, Inc, for the purpose of Atlanta's first municipal aviation field.

On April 20, 1925, Hartsfield was officially named the chairman of the city's new aviation committee by Mayor Sims to oversee the airport's operations. Hartsfield had already been working with Mayor Sims establishing early airport operations for approximately two years.

In December of 1925, Hartsfield, hoping that Candler would eventually donate the land to the city, introduced a motion to name the site Candler Field, after the former Mayor and Coca-Cola tycoon, Asa Candler.

Much of the early airport history is unclear because there are few records of the beginning of operations. However, just hours after the ink dried on the lease, grading of the Candler land began. Hartsfield had previously introduced surveys stating that the entire grading project could be completed for approximately $5,000. Hartsfield stated that he had workers on the field eight hours before funds were approved by the city.

one man said the planes frightened his cows

The idea of the city operating an airport brought much concern from Atlanta citizens. Many felt that the "airfield," as it was originally called, would be a real annoyance. One man said the planes frightened his cows! They even caused them to drop their calves too soon and to quit giving milk. Hartsfield

Photo: Courtesy of Ray Leader, Federal Aviation Administration (Retired), Hartsfield-Jackson Atlanta International Airport. Atlanta Airport (circa 1920's)

asked him how much he wanted for the pasture that adjoined the airfield. The man said one "thousand dollars." The city bought his land and a few years later sold part of it for $400,000.

Others argued that the city had no right to spend taxpayer money on airfields used primarily by rich sportsmen and young maniacs determined to break their necks. Hartsfield soothed them noting that the city was not paying anything for the property and had even persuaded the county to forego the taxes during the first five years.

he was ahead of nearly everybody in the United States

As Atlanta started using the airport, Hartsfield seemed to always be in the middle of anything and everything concerning the airport. Harold Sheats, a one time city attorney for the City of East Point and later the Fulton County Attorney, recalled that Hartsfield had the vision of Atlanta being an air center. "He was far ahead of his time…he was ahead of nearly everybody in the United States on aviation." When Atlanta started operating the airport, it consisted of a dirt runway. It was "a crude affair with one or two old garages and maybe a dozen WWI planes," Sheats remembered. [3]

John Ottley, an *Atlanta Journal* reporter and a member of the Junior Chamber Aviation Committee, once said, "I think Mayor Hartsfield did more for aviation than any one individual. When he was

3. Ibid. Living Atlanta p. 323

in the City Council, he recognized what it would mean to have Atlanta an air center as it was a rail center." Ottley, who would later become an airline executive, also recalled that "in the late twenties, Hartsfield led the effort to get the new southern airmail route through Atlanta." Ottley also said, "Secretary of Commerce McCracken came south to look into the terminus of a New York-Southeast line. Birmingham was all set up for it. And he just agreed to come through Atlanta and sort of say hello and look things over, but it was really all set for Birmingham. So Mayor Hartsfield (who at the time was an alderman) was responsible for getting Mr. McCracken and various prominent people in Atlanta together..."[4]

4. Ibid. Living Atlanta p. 93

Hartsfield was outraged to learn of this plan

The air mail route had already been put into place by federal officials from New York to Birmingham to Miami, and from Jacksonville to Birmingham to Chicago. Hartsfield was outraged to learn they had bypassed Atlanta. That's when he persuaded city officials to invite Secretary McCracken and other federal officials to take a look at Atlanta's airport.

They planned for the postal service to use Birmingham as a transfer point to handle the ever increasing airmail. Because radar and other navigation features used today were not yet invented, the federal government was planning to

Courtesy of the Atlanta Hartsfield-Jackson International Airport. First passengers into Candler Field Atlanta Airport 1930

Chapter 3 - The History of the Airport

install lighted and flashing beacons along the air route. (Some evidence of these early beacon towers were still around in the 1980's in locations like Cartersville, GA, and Stone Mountain, GA.)

Hartsfield made sure that Secretary McCracken and the other federal officials got a grand welcome in Atlanta. This included a police escort through the city, an elaborate dinner with some of the city's top businessmen, and all the pomp and circumstance that Hartsfield became known for as a City of Atlanta official.

Atlanta got the airmail route! This was a HUGE accomplishment for the new airfield. Hartsfield cheerfully stated throughout his career that Atlanta had "stolen" Birmingham's key position in the southern mail routes. However, it would probably be more accurate to say that Atlanta had pushed for the routes more than Birmingham did.

Existing documents include only vague details about how Atlanta obtained its airmail routes. In addition to Hartsfield, Senator Walter George, Congressman W. B. Upshaw, and Postmaster E. K. Large, all clearly played a role in Atlanta being chosen to implement the airmail routes through the south.

With the beacon lighted airmail routes now secured, Hartsfield looked at other ways to improve the new airport. His enthusiasm for the airport and its growth began to rub off on others. He would go out to the airport on the weekends and help keep the

Courtesy of the Atlanta Hartsfield-Jackson International Airport. Senator Walter F. George, W. K. Large, Atlanta Postmaster, and Alderman W. B. Hartsfield (circa 1930's)

Courtesy of the Atlanta Hartsfield-Jackson International Airport. W. K. Large returning from the first airmail flight out of the Atlanta airport (circa 1930's)

crowds in order. In those days, it was difficult to tell where the dirt runways ended and the parking areas began. The excited motorists would sometimes drive right out in front of taxiing planes.

The dirt runways usually caused problems for people living in nearby Hapeville. In 2012, I spoke with W. F. Whitton, my 92-year-old father-in-law, who lived with his father just two blocks from Candler Field when he was a child. At his age, his mind was still sharp and remembered that "the dust from the airplanes taking off would cover houses some two to three blocks away."

Pitcairn Aviation built the first hangers at Candler Field in 1927. Pitcairn would later change their name to Eastern Airlines. In 1928, Pitcairn won the airmail contract from the federal government, and began flying the airmail through Atlanta on May 1st of that year.

However, the first airmail flight out of Atlanta had been on September 15, 1926. Atlanta aviation history was made that day when a contract air mail carrier (called a CAM), that was leased to Florida Airways, Inc., took off bound for Miami with stops along the way scheduled for Macon, Georgia, Jacksonville, Tampa, and Fort Myers, Florida. The pilot, Ben Eilson, was told of a problem in Macon before leaving Atlanta. The airport there was being

Chapter 3 - The History of the Airport

Courtesy of the Atlanta Hartsfield-Jackson International Airport (circa 1940's)

plowed and he would not be able to land there, but he was to drop a bag of mail there. A pre-arranged sign was worked out between the postmasters in both cities. The Macon postmaster was to wave white handkerchiefs in each hand to signal Eilson. The mail drop was successful as Eilson flew over the Macon airfield. Those kind of airmail drops would not be allowed in today's more elaborate and sophisticated aviation centers.

That airmail route was discontinued in December of 1926, due to the lack of mail being delivered. The ten cents per ounce fee was significantly higher than fees of regular mail service. At the time, there were twelve air mail routes operational in the United States. The Atlanta to Miami route was the first route to fail.

In the late 1920's, Hartsfield urged the city to build a two-story building for eight thousand dollars on the airport property. He convinced the city that federal aviation officials should be offered rent free space in the building. This also helped promote the new airmail business in Atlanta.

The potential advantages of the airport were being noticed by many of the businessmen in Atlanta. Carling Dinkler, an Atlanta hotel manager, began to offer a free night stay for anyone coming into Atlanta by air travel.

1927 was a BIG year

1927 was a BIG year in the life of the new Atlanta airport! Charles Lindbergh came to Atlanta on his tour across the country after being the first person to successfully fly across the Atlantic nonstop in his plane, "The Spirit of St. Louis." He was not a stranger to Georgia, as he had made his first solo flight in May of 1923 from Souther Field in Americus, Georgia.

Many prominent people turned out to see Charles Lindbergh at the celebration in Atlanta. Hartsfield, who was only an alderman at the time, was not a part of the official welcoming committee, even though he made sure that he was in the midst of the proceedings. Hartsfield became known for not only putting the city's best foot forward, but most definitely his own. Behind the police escort, he rode as an escort in an open car (now called a convertible), along with the Atlanta Fire Chief

William B. Cody. Hartsfield waved jovially at the large crowd that had assembled to see Lindberg. Lindberg's visit to Atlanta was an exciting time for the city as well as the young airport.

the first ever true runway lights

Night flying had begun which was another intriguing development in 1927. Hartsfield was determined that Atlanta would be a world class around-the-clock airport. He traveled with R. C. Turner, a City of Atlanta electrician, around the country searching for specific lights that would work as runway lights. In 1927, night flying was uncommon to say the least. Some airfields had crude lighting systems which were insufficient in lighting a runway. Hartsfield finally decided to create his own runway lights. He chose a huge curved lens that had been developed in Holland and was sold in the states by General Electric.

Some say that the lights developed by Hartsfield and the electrician, R. C. Turner, were the first ever true runway lights. Soon, airport officials from all around the country were coming to Atlanta to see the Candler Field runway lights. In 1928, the Atlanta Chamber of Commerce awarded its Certificate of

Courtesy of Monty Cheshire, grandson of W. B. Hartsfield. Picture of Charles A. Lingbergh given to Alderman Hartsfield after his famous flight, 1927

Courtesy of Ray Leader, Federal Aviation Administration (Retired), Hartsfield-Jackson Atlanta International Airport. Many attended the dedication of the new 1939 control tower at the Atlanta Airport

Distinguished Achievement to Hartsfield for developing the lighting system at the Atlanta airport.

Hartsfield took a hands-on approach to early aviation in Atlanta! He did everything including repairing planes, inspecting hangers and promoting the barnstormers. Barnstormers was a name given to early aviators who were dare devils that would literally fly through open barn doors in their small planes. People would even buy tickets to ride with the barnstormers from Candler Field. I can't imagine what they were thinking!

Hartsfield was among several including Harold Sheets, John Ottley, an Atlanta Journal reporter, and Roscoe Turner, an early noted speed flyer, who made a historic flight from Atlanta. It was the first flight from Atlanta to New York combining airmail with passengers. It was a publicity stunt to say the least. Included in the mail was a check for a million dollars that was being transferred from Atlanta to the Federal Reserve Bank in New York.

Roscoe Turner flew the plane that ended up crashing in a farmer's backyard in Abbeville, South Carolina. A Fox newsreel cameraman was the first one off the ill fated flight. The story was told that the cameraman said to the farmer, "Don't be frightened. We just dropped in to pick a few apples." The farmer replied, "Sorry mister, they ain't ripe yet."[5]

5. Ibid. Living Atlanta p. 328

Hartsfield urged the city to buy

Hartsfield urged the city to buy the leased airfield in 1929, paying $94,000 for the 297 acre property from the Candler family. Later, two major airlines, Eastern Air Lines and Delta Air Lines both would use Atlanta as their chief hubs. Delta continues to use Atlanta as their chief hub and world wide headquarters. Eastern Air Lines was a major United States airline from 1926 to 1991 and was dissolved and ceased operations on January 18, 1991.

Eastern Air Lines had a rich and varied history. It's formation was a combination of several companies including Pitcairn Aviation, Inc. and Florida Airways. At one time, Eastern was owned by General Motors. Eddie Rickenbacker, a WWI flying ace and a Medal of Honor recipient, was both the president and part owner at one time.

In the late 1930's, Eastern's fleet of planes was called The Great Silver Fleet. Pictures from the inaugural flight of the Great Silver Fleet out of Atlanta are shown on the next page. Eddie Rickenbacker was almost killed in an Eastern plane crash approaching Atlanta near Jonesboro, Georgia, in 1941.

The Atlanta Airport, as it has been called by many over the years, was a busy airport from its inception. By the end of 1930, it placed third in the nation behind New York City and Chicago. Atlanta's regular daily flights totalled sixteen (yes, only sixteen) arriving and departing in 1930. In 2014, the official Atlanta airport website indicates that 2,500 flights arrive and depart daily. [6]

6. www.Atlanta-Airport.com

Courtesy of Ray Leader, Federal Aviation Administration (Retired), Hartsfield-Jackson Atlanta International Airport. Atlanta Airport (circa 1940's)

Chapter 3 - The History of the Airport

Courtesy of Tom Dorsett who is a retired aviator with several private corporations. I met Tom while teaching a class about the Atlanta airport at Kennesaw State Continuing Education in 2012 (circa 1930's)

Courtesy of Monty Cheshire, grandson of W. B. Hartsfield. William B. Hartsfield's on Eastern Airlines Inaugural flight, New York-Brownsville-Mexico, D.F. Set for takeoff from Atlanta! Mayor Hartsfield third on left (circa 1930's)

Eastern Air Lines Picture, Courtesy of Monty Cheshire

Prior to take off on the first flight of the Silver Fleet from Atlanta Municipal Airport, to New York, Brownsville, Texas and on to Mexico (circa 1930's)

(L to R) A. B. Landa, attorney, Washington D. C.; John Farber, attorney, New York; Jesse Briegel, attorney, New York; Ralph McGill, executive editor, Atlanta Constitution; V. C. Chenea, general traffic manager, Pan American Airways, New York City; Capt. Eddie Rickenbacker, President and General Manager, Eastern Air Lines; William K. Jenkins, L. and J. Theatres Co., Atlanta, Ga.; (Standing on steps of plane) Jesse Draper, chairman of Atlanta Aviation Committee, Alvin B. Cates, President, Atlanta Chamber of Commerce; Mayor Ben E. Douglas, Charlotte N. C,; Mayor William B. Hartsfield, Atlanta, Ga.; Wiley L. Moore, President, Wofford Oil Co., and director of Eastern Air Lines, Atlanta, Ga.; Robert Ramspeck, member of Congress, Atlanta, Ga.; Paul H. Brattain, First Vice President, Eastern Air Lines, New York; Smythe Gambrell, Eastern Air Lines attorney, Atlanta, Ga.; R. W. Courts, Jr., Atlanta broker; Don Luis Quintanilla, Minister Resident and Charge d-Affairs, Mexican Embassy, Washington, D.C.; and Salvandor Duhart, second secretary, Mexican Embassy, Washington, D. C.

The Atlanta Aircraft Corporation was an aircraft manufacturer in 1929. Charles Lindbergh stated that their planes were "ten years ahead of its time." Two of the owners of the Atlanta Aircraft Corporation were Ernest Woodruff, the Coca Cola tycoon, and William C. Wardlaw, an Atlanta banker. The stock market crash of 1929 helped bring about the collapse of this corporation.

Airport Manager Jack Gray

Hartsfield and Jack Gray, the airport manager from 1929-1962, worked tirelessly on the early airport's inception and growth. Both were visionary's who transformed the old Candler race track into the world's busiest airport. One of his colleagues said, "Gray was a man who let few obstacles get in his way."

Ray Nixon, the Director of Public Works for the City of Atlanta for thirty plus years, once said, "Gray was a pretty hard bargainer and he existed out there on his ability to rustle stuff up." [7] Gray often did what ever it took to help make the airport grow, which included using prison labor for surveying and extending the runways.

In 1934, Beeler Blevins and Doug Davis, two of Atlanta's early aviation heros, lost their lives. Blevins died from injuries sustained in an automobile accident on Stewart Avenue (now called Metropolitan Avenue), just a few miles from the airport. Davis crashed in Cleveland, Ohio, at the annual National Air Races, less than four months later.

By 1935, the Federal Government had contributed more than a half million dollars to the Atlanta

7. Ibid. A Dream Takes Flight p. 61

Courtesy of Ray Leader, Federal Aviation Administration (Retired), Hartsfield-Jackson Atlanta International Airport. Atlanta Airport (circa 1950's)

Courtesy of Ray Leader, Federal Aviation Administration (Retired), Hartsfield-Jackson Atlanta International Airport. Atlanta Airport (circa 1940's)

airport. By today's standards that does not sound like a lot of money, but in the early 1930's, a half million dollars contributed greatly to the airport's early development. In 1935, President Roosevelt created the Works Progress Administration (WPA). This agency was designed to help airports grow their manpower, offer engineering expertise and appropriate necessary funds that would be used to improve and expand the nation's airports.

During 1935, the three Atlanta runways were paved and widened to 150 feet, which was more than adequate for the needs of the day. Most international airports today have runways approximately 200 feet wide.

In June of 1935, Eddie Rickenbacker, Eastern Airlines President, led the transfer of the carrier's headquarters to Miami, although Atlanta remained a hub for Eastern. In 1935, Delta began planning to move its headquarters to Atlanta from Monroe, Louisiana. It took a few years to complete this move.

By 1936, Atlanta's runway structure consisted of three paved strips with the longest being 3,500 feet.

Hartsfield was elected Mayor of Atlanta in 1937

Hartsfield was elected Mayor of Atlanta in 1937. Jack Gray and Hartsfield became powerful allies in the continued development of the airport. George Goodwin, a public relations executive and civic organizer, once said, "Hartsfield was one of the really big keys to developing the field because he understood the federal government and how it operated. He had the biggest ears and the fastest feet I've ever seen. If he heard that there was

Chapter 3 - The History of the Airport

Courtesy of Ray Leader, Federal Aviation Administration (Retired), Hartsfield-Jackson Atlanta International Airport. Atlanta Airport (circa 1940's)

some money that Atlanta might get for the airport, or some other project, he would get himself or someone else up to Washington and convince them that the money should come here." [8]

Jack Gray announced, in May of 1937, that the east-west runway would be expanded an additional 2,000 feet making it a total of 4,600 feet. The WPA funded this expansion due primarily to Gray's work with them. In the fall of 1937, Hartsfield pressed the federal government for legislation to make loans and grants to cities to enlarge and modernize their airports.

The original control tower at Candler Field was opened in March of 1939. An administration wing

8. Ibid. A Dream Takes Flight p. 95

was included in the six story facility used for much needed office space. The control tower cost approximately $27,000 to build.

A national air traffic control network went into effect October 1939. The Atlanta tower was one of the first to be operated by the CAA, Civil Aeronautics Administration. It was the predecessor of what is now the Federal Aviation Administration or FAA. The FAA, like the airport, has had several different names.

In 1939, Gray backed by Hartsfield, proposed a fourth runway. In a proposal to the CAA, Atlanta wanted to construct a fourth northeast-southwest runway that would be 3,200 feet long. They also wanted to extend the northwest-southeast runway to 6,000 feet making it comparable to other runways in the country. Needless to say, it was an ambitious proposal that would also require some 260 acres of additional land which was almost equal to the original size of the airport. The CAA was proposing to congress that key airports begin to expand for military readiness as Great Britain and France declared war on Germany in September of 1939. This was the beginning of the largest building boom to date at Atlanta's airport. The airport was now close to fifteen years old.

During the American build-up to World War II, the military began using Candler Field. In fact, the United States government declared it a military airfield. Beginning in 1940, the United States Air Force operated it as Atlanta Army Airfield simultaneously with Candler Field. Atlanta Army Airfield was never an official name, although it was called this by the military.

The Air Force used the airport mostly for the servicing of transient planes, including many different types of combat aircraft that were being maintained at the airport during and before World War II. The airport doubled in size during the war. It set a record for takeoffs and landings in a single day during the war, making it the nation's busiest airport in terms of flight operation. This trend has continued to the present day. In a single day, there were over 1,700 flights in and out of the airport.

Mayor Hartsfield and Jack Gray had lured an Army reserve squadron to Atlanta years earlier. This paid off with the war build up in 1940. The city had

Courtesy of the Atlanta Hartsfield-Jackson International Airport. (circa 1940's). Atlanta's first tower is the middle white building at bottom of photo

Chapter 3 - The History of the Airport

gained priority in requesting WPA construction funds. Hartsfield and Gray worked the Federal Government in applying for numerous defense funds, thereby helping the airport to grow considerably during the war years.

On the political front, Mayor Hartsfield lost his only election that fall and Roy LeCraw became the Mayor for a short time before resigning to join the Army.

Delta makes Atlanta their home

Despite a few bumps during the war years, the airport's growth continued. Delta helped as well by officially making Atlanta their new headquarters on March 1, 1941. Hartsfield and Gray had been working with Delta for several years. Some said that Delta may have made their home here because of Hartsfield and Gray. As a member of the Hartsfield family, I have heard that all my life. Unfortunately, I could find no official records to substantiate that claim. But according to members of the family, Hartsfield definitely had something to do with Delta making Atlanta their home.

The CAA held its first tower controller school in Atlanta during November and December of 1941. The city's tower was the first in the country to be converted to federal operation.

In 1942, the airport collected more revenue than it dispensed for the first time. The total amount collected was $30,477 with only $27,926 paid out.

Delta Air Lines developed a group of female mechanics due to many men going into the military or working civilian government jobs. Their reser-

Courtesy of Ray Leader, Federal Aviation Administration (Retired), Hartsfield-Jackson Atlanta International Airport. Atlanta Airport (circa 1940's)

Courtesy of Ray Leader, Federal Aviation Administration (Retired), Hartsfield-Jackson Atlanta International Airport. Atlanta Airport (circa 1940's)

vation force became almost exclusively female. Before the war it was mostly male.

A new lighting system and instrument landing system were both installed in 1942, costing approximately $100,000, with the CAA picking up the tab. During that year, many lobby and administration office improvements were put into place.

In July of 1944, Southern Airways completed a new $100,000 hanger. It was said to be the largest privately owned structure in the country.

By 1944, more than $2.3 million had been spent in developing Atlanta's airport with more than $1.4 million of that coming from the federal government. The land area of the airport now totalled 1,240 acres. Remember, at the beginning, it was thought that "no airfield would ever need more than 200 acres."

Atlanta Army Airfield ceased operations after the war ended. The use of the airport for national defense and the funds provided by the federal government had contributed to tremendous growth at the Atlanta airport.

people still called it Candler Field

In 1942, Candler Field was renamed Atlanta Municipal Airport. Due to poor record keeping, several different stories emerged regarding the time when the name was changed. Some records show the city passed two separate ordinances changing the name to the Atlanta Municipal Airport before then. Other records indicated that the name was changed as early as 1929, when Hartsfield was an alderman. Hartsfield recalled the official name change taking place in 1929. The name had been so ingrained in the minds of Atlantans, that people continued to call it Candler Field up to 1942.

Chapter 3 - The History of the Airport

Courtesy of Ray Leader, Federal Aviation Administration (Retired), Hartsfield-Jackson Atlanta International Airport. Atlanta Airport (circa 1940's).

When the United States Post Office opened its airport branch in 1942, it was called The Candler Field Post Office. This stunned Mayor Hartsfield and Airport Manager Jack Gray. They protested to the post office, but as was often the case in early airport history, no record of the name change could be found in council records.

With the war over, the federal funds dried up. The airport was still growing as more and more passenger flights used the airport. Commercial jets were just a few years away. Hartsfield and Gray, along with other officials, knew that they were going to need a larger terminal. With money tight, the two came up with a plan.

They planned to develop one of the abandoned government hangers into a new terminal buying some time before they would have to build a new terminal. Hartsfield had heard that the New Orleans airport had done something similar earlier. In fact, he and several other's, including Jack Gray and George Goodwin, an ***Atlanta Journal*** reporter, drove to New Orleans to see how they had transformed their army hanger into a terminal. Members of the city council were concerned that a converted hanger would reflect adversely on Atlanta's image. With some deluxe interior features planned, skeptics were kept at bay. The old hanger was developed over the next couple of years into an attractive and functional passenger terminal at the low price of $270,000.

Hartsfield, always the master of ceremonies, hosted over 175 officials at the opening of the terminal on May 9, 1948. Delta's President C. E. Woolman and Eastern's Eddie Rickenbacker were among the dignitaries that were present.

In 1948, more than a million passengers passed

through the new terminal building, which once served as the WWII surplus hangar. Atlanta's new terminal displayed the longest ticket counter in the world. Hartsfield's idea was to add an observation deck across the front of the terminal. The airport charged ten cents per person to go out on the observation deck. The airport collected more than $7,500 during the first seven months the observation deck was open. That was more than half the cost to build the deck.

airplanes were still a novelty to most people

Parents brought their children to gaze at the activity on the field and couples would catch the breeze during the twilight hours. Airplanes were still a novelty to most people. Despite continuous growth of aviation, still more than three fourths of the country's population had never flown.

In 1948, ground breaking took place on the new runway system as part of the 1944 master site plan. The existing four runways would be replaced by three longer ones. MacDougald Construction Company of Atlanta won the bid for construction and paving with the low bid of $1,121,584. The three new runways would be 6,000 feet, 6,000 feet and 7,200 feet. Construction of the new runways had to carry on around the active four shorter runways. The lighting and electrical installation bid was won by Harrison-Wright Company of Charlotte at $63,834.

About the same time, the CAA installed the South's first improved ground control approach radar

Courtesy of Ray Leader, Federal Aviation Administration (Retired), Hartsfield-Jackson Atlanta International Airport. Atlanta Airport (circa 1940's)

system for a mere $150,000. This system helped eliminate many fog and cloud related difficulties as well as radar "ground clutter" (false signals from reflections on buildings). This new system was an immense help to Atlanta's air traffic controllers.

The airport growth sky rocketed along with airline profits. Delta spent over a million dollars in 1947 expanding its Atlanta headquarters and maintenance shops. Southern Airways labored anxiously striving to complete its financing. They had to begin operating by the June 10th deadline that had been set by the CAA. Southern Airways barely accomplished the deadline.

Private flying kept pace with the commercial side. In 1949, Fulton County began construction on a new airport west of town to handle the ever increasing general aviation. The airport was called Fulton County Airport – Brown Field, named for Charlie Brown, who was the Atlanta area politician who ran against Mayor Hartsfield three times.

By 1949, more than 700 daily flights (including general aviation and military flights) were departing or landing at Atlanta Municipal Airport. These statistics ranked Atlanta fourth in the nation at that time.

passenger traffic had jumped to 1.4 million

In 1952, passenger traffic jumped to 1.4 million travelers a year, a 500% increase over 1941 totals. Southern Airways was now flying to 33 cities and pressing to add even more routes.

Delta merged with Chicago and Southern Airways in 1953. Arguments began around this time for a second Atlanta airport because of the continued growth, but of course this never happened.

Courtesy of Ray Leader, Federal Aviation Administration (Retired), Hartsfield-Jackson Atlanta International Airport. Atlanta Airport (circa 1940's)

In 1953, Jack Gray celebrated his 25th year as the airport manager. Grady Ridgeway was hired by the airport in 1954 and was named the assistant airport manager the following year.

Eastern and Delta were vying for control in Atlanta. Eastern was operating more flights out of Atlanta in 1955 than all of the other airlines combined just ten years earlier. The success of the two airlines was both good and bad for the Atlanta airport. Both airlines considered various ways to help their respective businesses while still looking out for the Atlanta airport.

now the terminal was estimated to cost some six million

Courtesy of Ray Leader, Federal Aviation Administration-Retired, Hartsfield-Jackson Atlanta International Airport. 1954 Aerial

Despite the deluxe features, the old surplus terminal was not able to keep up with the demands of a fast growing aviation center. Something had to be done. Eastern's Eddie Rickenbacker was so frustrated by the choking growth that he offered to build a new terminal just for Eastern passengers. Without question, Atlanta was going to have to construct a new terminal, as well as add additional office spaces, maintenance facilities, and once again improve runways as well as paved taxi runway areas. In 1952, the new airport terminal was estimated to cost $3 million. In 1956, the ground had not even been broken. By then, the terminal was estimated to cost approximately $6 million. Additional improvements would drive the cost to over $14 million.

Mayor Hartsfield did not believe that the city should be responsible for paying all the costs. Beginning in 1952, he was the leader of the American Municipal Association, known as the mayor's mayor. He assisted mayors across the country with capital improvements for their respective cities and airports. He fought vigorously to get financial assistance from the federal government and felt strongly that the government should help finance airports or at least defray the cost.

Hartsfield wanted the federal dollars but also knew he had to convince local investors that they would benefit from airport improvements. In addition, he worked with local government officials in putting bonds in place to raise additional funds. Hartsfield had done such a good job with Atlanta finances

Courtesy of Tom Dorsett who is a retired aviator with several private corporations. I met Tom while teaching a class about the Atlanta airport at Kennesaw State Continuing Education in 2012. (circa 1950's)

over the years, the bonds would come with very favorable rates.

Compounding the need for additional financing and necessary improvements at the airport was the fact that we were entering the jet age. Eastern and Delta had already begun studying plans for new jet aircraft and maintenance facilities.

A new terminal was well into the planning stages, but the current terminal had reached critical conditions. Additions and improvements would have to be made to keep it safe and functional. The airlines and the city had to construct concourses or "fingers" that were temporarily made only of wood. The airport's continual growth demanded more usable space which made it extremely difficult to wait on the forthcoming terminal. These expensive improvements to the terminal cost more than $800,000 and would only be temporary. The additions would be torn down in just a few short years.

Maneuvering airplanes around crowded gates became hazardous at the old terminal. Passengers arriving at the terminal encountered obstacles due to the narrow overcrowded streets in the City of Hapeville. This was the main route to the existing terminal crossing over a busy rail line leading to the Atlanta Ford Assembly Plant. At that time, getting to the airport was problematic as was boarding from the terminal.

A new entrance to the airport had been needed for

several years. In fact, what was needed was a multi-lane road that would link Atlanta to the airport and the proposed expressways. These plans had been discussed as early as 1946. Four different routes had been recommended by the city, state, county and metropolitan planning commission. Like the airport, funds for new road construction were short as well.

Somehow it all began to fall into place. County, city and federal governments all played a part in the planning of the new entrance to the airport. In 1955, the federal funding of the new interstate highway system was announced and the plan was for a new interstate highway to come within a quarter of a mile of the ever growing airport. Now, the city could afford to build a road to connect the airport with the new highway and it quickly gained support of all involved. The entrance to the airport changed several times over the years. It was first routed from the City of Hapeville. Later a new entrance was added off of Virginia Avenue. In 1980, the main entrance became Camp Creek Parkway with the opening of the midfield terminal.

Courtesy of Ray Leader, Federal Aviation Administration (Retired), Hartsfield-Jackson Atlanta International Airport. 1959 Aerial

the first international flight ever made out of Atlanta

On June 1, 1956, an Eastern Airlines flight to Montreal, Canada, was the first scheduled international flight ever made out of Atlanta. In 1957, Atlanta's first jet flight passed through the expanding airport. Work would soon begin on the new terminal to help alleviate the congestion that had become a part of the early airport. Atlanta became the busiest airport in the country with more than two million passengers passing through in 1957. Also in 1957, it became the busiest airport in the world between the hours of noon and 2 p.m. daily.

In October of 1958, the city advertised for construction bids for the newly proposed terminal.

Sixteen companies placed bids. Blount Brothers of Montgomery, Alabama, narrowly won the bidding process with the low bid of $9,996,000. On December 15, 1958, the city board of aldermans unanimously voted to accept the bid and Mayor Hartsfield signed it immediately. It was the largest single expenditure in Atlanta history at that point. The bid was reduced to $9,677,889 according to an *Atlanta Constitution* story on December 16th.

Ed Moulthrop, an architect with Robert and Company, designed what was called the 1961 terminal. He said "Hartsfield was ahead of his time in thinking that America's great cities would be based on aviation. He believed that a city's position as an aviation center determined its commercial growth...." [9]

Ed Moulthrop also believed that Delta President, C. E. Woolman, convinced the other airlines that despite its cost, the new terminal had to be built.

During the building of the terminal, there were multiple construction problems. Union disputes slowed the building process several times. Because of the labor problems, the scheduled completion was pushed from January to February to the spring.

On May 3, 1961, the new terminal opened. Instantly, it became the largest in the country, able to accommodate more than 6 million travelers a year. While most marveled and praised the terminal, Jack Gray, the airport manager, told Mayor Hartsfield that the terminal was already obsolete and would not be able to handle the crowds. Obviously, neither Hartsfield nor incoming Mayor Ivan Allen wanted to hear that. However, Gray's prediction rang true when the new terminal was stretched beyond its capacity the very first year. Over 9.5 million people passed through the new terminal of which 3.8 million were actual passengers.

9. Ibid. A Dream Takes Flight p. 95

Courtesy of the Atlanta Hartsfield-Jackson International Airport. (circa 1960s)

Courtesy of the Atlanta Hartsfield-Jackson International Airport (circa 1960s) Entrance into the 1961 terminal off of Virginia Ave.

Atlantans will remember as the turquoise terminal

Most travelers and Atlantans will remember the new terminal as the turquoise terminal. The terminal opened after Mayor Hartsfield left office as mayor. Mayor Allen would continue with the advancement of the airport during his administration as Atlanta's new mayor. With everything from site preparation, furnishings and more, the terminal ended up costing the city approximately $21 million.

The terminal was beautiful and known for its gleaming turquoise exterior and enormous arches at the entrance. The interior included a spacious lighted atrium lobby, a full 500 foot ticketing counter, stunning gift shops, newsstands, restaurants and much more. For its time, it was extravagant for the Atlanta airport and outshined any previous architecture. The new parking area consisted of over 4,500 spaces. This was a vast improvement from the original war surplus hangar which served as the terminal for twelve years and only had a couple of hundred parking spaces.

Shortly after the opening of the new airport terminal, Jack Gray followed Hartsfield in retirement. He had served the airport for more than thirty-two years. Hartsfield and Gray had "built" the airport from its dark days of the 1930's when money was tight. The airports growth was due primarily to their perseverance and tenacity. These two pioneers brought the airport from post World War II days to national prominence and into the jet age.

Grady Ridgeway took over the reigns of the airport in mid 1961. In the early sixties, airplanes had improved becoming a more desirable, comfortable and faster form of travel, which enticed more people to fly. As good as this was for the Atlanta airport, it certainly brought added traffic issues. With the jet age here, runways would have to be lengthened

Courtesy of Ray Leader, Federal Aviation Administration (Retired), Hartsfield-Jackson Atlanta International Airport. (circa 1960's)

to accommodate the larger, more sophisticated jets. Once again, congestion in Atlanta meant that the airport and the runway system would have to be enlarged and improved.

The runway system that was being used (similar to an A pattern) was inefficient and allowed only one plane at a time to land. In 1961, there were 524 scheduled flights a day, plus other non-scheduled flights. Parallel runways were desperately needed.

The new airport leadership consisting of Mayor Allen, Airport Manager Grady Ridgeway, and Alderman Richard Freeman, head of the aviation committee, would now have to deal with a new runway design and construction that would mean acquiring more land. The new runways would cost almost $20 million. Due to increasing airport noise, the airport was already receiving complaints and lawsuits from nearby residents. And now they would need additional land and finances for future growth.

With much excitement, Mayor Allen announced in April of 1963, that the city would extend the present east west runway from 7,860 feet to 8,875 feet. They would also build a parallel 10,000 foot runway which would suffice for even the largest commercial jets. However, the plan had to be changed after the FAA and the Air Line Pilots Association (ALPA) questioned the proposed runway separations. In the final plan, the existing runway was lengthened to 10,000 feet and the new runway was only 8,000 feet. That runway would prove to be too short and within two years the airport was planning to lengthen it. However, that extension did not begin until 1984.

the stress on Atlanta's airport facilities had grown

In 1963, Delta would board more than a million passengers in Atlanta (the first carrier to ever board that number in a single year). 1964 would prove to be a banner year for all the carriers in Atlanta. But in 1964, the stress on Atlanta's airport facilities had grown once again into what had been a continual dilemma. The airport had always suffered from a lack of funds which had caused a lack of planning. Plans had to be short term to take care of current challenges. Due to lack of funds, planning for 15-20 years into the future was not typical. Despite short term continual planning, it seemed the city had not considered the long range planning that was required for the enormous airport growth.

over $170 million dollars had been spent on the airport

Airport officials were familiar with this scenario. There was talk of a second airport once again. Up to that date, over $170 million dollars had been spent on the airport operations. However, that was minuscule compared to what would be spent in the near future. Airports nationwide had grown into massive complexities costing millions of dollars each time there were major expansions.

Courtesy of Ray Leader, Federal Aviation Administration (Retired), Hartsfield-Jackson Atlanta International Airport. The turquoise terminal from 1961 to 1980

Chapter 3 - The History of the Airport

The airlines were desperate for more gate space. Air traffic controllers were frequently busy with stacking planes in a holding pattern trying to land and take off at Atlanta's crowded airport. Plans were put into place for enlarging the 1961 terminal to 88 gates through multi-gate rotundas at the end of each concourse.

The newly formed municipal advisory group called the Atlanta Region Metropolitan Planning Commission (ARMPC) began a two year study that looked at the future over the next three decades. After several revisions, plans included a midfield terminal which would add two additional parallel runways. Atlanta would now become a super airport and not require a second airport at this time. Also, cargo and maintenance hangers would have to be moved away from the passenger terminal.

Recommendations contained in the study included the purchase of some 900 nearby homes and over 1,200 additional acres. Implementation would require moving five to seven schools and a cemetery. The study certainly had its critics.

New federal regulations now mandated FAA approved master plans before federal funds would be granted. The FAA had notified Atlanta officials that a lack of an approved plan was putting present and future federal funds in jeopardy. It was now imperative that the city, the airlines, and the FAA reach some sort of agreement. Officials, unable to accomplish this, looked to an outside mediator.

Courtesy of Ray Leader, Federal Aviation Administration (Retired), Hartsfield-Jackson Atlanta International Airport. 1957 Aerial view shows construction of the 1961 terminal at the top of the photo

Courtesy of Ray Leader, Federal Aviation Administration (Retired), Hartsfield-Jackson Atlanta International Airport. 1954 Aerial

Paul Pate, a Delta vice president, recommended Leigh Fisher, who was one of the most respected airport consultants in the nation. On June 1, 1966, Fisher and officials signed a letter of agreement to allow Fisher to submit a plan referred to as the work program report. In it, he reinforced the ARMPC conclusion that Atlanta's main airport should remain where it was.

Fisher stated that it would be impossible to secure another site that was so closely located to the heart of the city and served by three interstate highways. Duplication of the airport infrastructure alone would prove to be too costly.

Atlanta's airport would be adequate

Fisher maintained that Atlanta's airport would be adequate with some proposed changes and additions if the flow of scheduled traffic were more even throughout the day. He suggested that a second or reliever airport could be built in the future which would be primarily for passengers starting or ending their travel in Atlanta. He believed that this airport should be on the north side of town. However, to date, city officials have never been able to agree on a site for the second airport although there have been several recommendations. The city of Atlanta has purchased land in Paulding and Forsyth counties that might be used for this purpose.

Fisher also confirmed that a third parallel runway south of the parallel runway of 1964 would vastly increase airport capacity. Fisher's plans guided the planning for the next fourteen years and included

Courtesy of Ray Leader, Federal Aviation Administration (Retired), Hartsfield-Jackson Atlanta International Airport. Atlanta terminal (circa 1970's)

Courtesy of Ray Leader, Federal Aviation Administration (Retired), Hartsfield-Jackson Atlanta International Airport. Passenger arrival and departure location at 1961 terminal (circa 1970's)

developing the airport to the maximum extent possible.

From September 1966 to March 1967, city and airline officials along with Fisher revised and refined his work into the master plan for airport development. Fisher had recommended hiring a coordinator who would oversee both the technical and administrative sides of the expansions. That coordinator would also manage a council of local governments to deal with inevitable frictions of airport expansion. Maxwell W. Walker was hired for this position in June of 1967 and served the expansion project for the next thirteen years.

In 1967, the city of Atlanta and the airlines began to work on a master plan for forthcoming growth and development of the Atlanta Municipal Airport. Because of the urgent need by the airlines to acquire more gate space and another runway, the airlines agreed to an unprecedented plan to finance the land needed. This, of course, was usually the most time-consuming step in any airport expansion.

In November of 1967, it was announced that two architectural companies would work together to design the mid-field terminal. Atlanta based Stevens & Wilkinson would work with Detroit based Smith, Hinchman and Grylls, who had recently designed the new Detroit Metro Airport.

the current mid-field terminal of today

The consultation process by Fisher eventually became known as the 1968 Airport Layout Plan. In the plan, the airlines agreed to finance approximately half of the estimated expansion price of $164 million. This was the beginning of the current mid-field terminal of today.

Along with this plan, came studies and negotiations about whether to keep at least one crosswind runway. Critics said that Atlanta needed at least one north-south runway. In May of 1968, the FAA gave approval to do away with any crosswind runways as Atlanta planned a third east-west parallel runway.

Courtesy of Ray Leader, Federal Aviation Administration (Retired), Hartsfield-Jackson Atlanta International Airport. (circa 1960's)

Courtesy of Ray Leader, Federal Aviation Administration (Retired), Hartsfield-Jackson Atlanta International Airport. 1962 Atlanta Municipal Airport with terminal building in back left

Between November 1967 and late Summer 1968, Eastern Air Lines opened a $1.5 million automated cargo facility and began to expand and modernize its gates. Southern Airways was in the midst of a $2.5 million expansion of their aircraft maintenance hanger. Delta added their two six-gate "jet age" rotundas at the end of concourses E and F at a cost of about $7 million.

Plans for the new mid-field terminal were scheduled and then called off several times over the next few years. Officials struggled with costs, land acquisition, new federal runway regulations, and the airlines approval of multiple aspects of the proposed new terminal.

With the on and off plans to build, talks surfaced of a second airport once again. Meanwhile the 1961 terminal was extremely overcrowded and the northern most east-west runway was in need of repair after twenty years of heavy traffic. To buy time before the new terminal was started, the city approved a $2.73 million expansion that was to be finished by 1971.

Airport officials decided to completely reconstruct the runway with concrete, rather than the usual asphalt overlay. They would also put in new drainage and electrical systems. The job had to be done in no more than forty days, according to the bid that included penalties for every day over forty and a bonus for early completion. Three shifts worked around the clock and the miracle runway was competed in exactly forty days at a cost of over $7.7 million.

battle over the midfield terminal idea

The city and the airlines continued to battle over the idea of building a midfield terminal or building a new reliever airport. Meanwhile, proposed cost continued to skyrocket.

There were four proposed sites for a reliever airport. The case for expanding Atlanta Municipal Airport also continued. The politics of whether to expand or add a second airport continued into the new administration of Mayor Sam Massell in January of 1970. A new site in Dawson County was now being considered for a second reliever airport. Throughout 1970, the expansion idea also continued despite a short time when air traffic declined nationally due to the economy being in a recession.

Despite the recession, in September of 1970, Delta acquired Atlanta's first Boeing 747. Several other airlines were considering larger aircraft hoping the future would return increased passenger air travel.

On February 22, 1971, Mayor Hartsfield passed away. Mayor Sam Massell and the city aldermen voted to rename the airport "William B. Hartsfield Atlanta Airport." This was the third official name of the airport and the renaming took place just six days after Mayor Hartsfield's passing and one day before what would have been his 81st birthday.

Just four months later, July 1st, the airport had another "official" name change as the word international had to be added. It would now be called "William B. Hartsfield Atlanta International Airport." This became the fourth official name change for the 46 year old airport.

With the decline in air travel and the heavy financial losses of the airlines in the early 1970's, the airlines questioned the practicality of a second major airport for Atlanta before 1980.

Courtesy of Ray Leader, Federal Aviation Administration (Retired), Hartsfield-Jackson Atlanta International Airport. 1964 Aerial of Atlanta Municipal Airport

Courtesy of Ray Leader, Federal Aviation Administration (Retired), Hartsfield-Jackson Atlanta International Airport. 1962 Atlanta Municipal Airport, side view

Hartsfield airport was busting at the seams

Hartsfield airport was busting at the seams. The airlines again turned to the initial recommendation of the 1966-67 plan to continue to maximize the capacity of Hartsfield.

Max Walker had continued updating the airport layout plan and had even developed a process of completing the expansion in phases, with or without the financial aid of the airlines. The third parallel runway construction was underway and it was scheduled to be operational by early 1973.

Despite the plan to finally move forward to build the mid-field terminal and continue expanding Hartsfield, the Atlanta Board of Aldermen voted in May of 1972 to purchase the 10,130 acre site in Dawson County as a possible site for a second future airport. Deputy Airport Commissioner George Berry (who would become the Commissioner of Aviation in 1978) said it gave Atlanta an option for the future and the $5 million price tag was very reasonable for a tract of land that large.

With the third parallel runway opening in February 1973, the airport could now land two planes simultaneously. Also in 1973, Grady Ridgeway, the airport manager, sent the airport layout plan to the

FAA. He began to prepare, in conjunction with the Georgia Department of Transportation, to relocate Interstate 85.

In August, another possible second airport site materialized. Atlanta went on to purchase the site in Paulding and Polk counties in 1975, again seeking a possible future second airport site.

Maynard Jackson was elected

In 1974, Maynard Jackson was elected and became the first black Mayor of Atlanta. The Board of Alderman was reconstituted by a new city charter into the Atlanta City Council. In mid summer 1974, the airlines were once again enjoying a surge in air travel and the 1961 terminal was quickly returning to its over crowded state of a couple of years prior.

By August, Delta wanted to proceed with the mid-field terminal. United and Southern airlines agreed by mid October. The city was wary that the airlines would once again back down on their financial commitments to proceed, so the city asked for formal letters of intent to proceed by December 31, 1974. This time Eastern refused to participate financially. But by early 1975, Eastern surprised it's colleagues by joining them, not wanting to be left behind at the old terminal.

Discussions continued whether to build in increments or build as many gates as the airlines decreed. Only one barrier was left in continuing to move forward, which was a financial plan the airlines could afford. The carriers negotiated a series of second and third lien bonds with the city. With the financial details sorted out, mid-field construction could finally begin, or could it?

Courtesy of Ray Leader, Federal Aviation Administration (Retired), Hartsfield-Jackson Atlanta International Airport. Runway Aerial 1975

Courtesy of Ray Leader, Federal Aviation Administration (Retired), Hartsfield-Jackson Atlanta International Airport. Airport Aerial 1975

Mayor Jackson had different priorities. Jackson had campaigned on a platform that would give more black firms the opportunity to obtain city contracts. He demanded one fourth of all contracts go to minority firms, either directly, or through joint ventures with white-owned firms. Furthermore, he insisted that the minority partners be local.

Stevens and Wilkinson, the architectural firm, failed to respond to Jackson's demands quickly enough. It was reported that Jackson's former law partner David Franklin and Emma Darnell, Jackson's executive assistant, telephoned the firm with threats to cancel their contract. The firm's airport project director, Minton Braddy, called the pressure "blackmail." Braddy was fired after his comments were reported in the September issue of the ***Atlanta Journal-Constitution Magazine.***

Both Mayor Jackson and Stevens and Wilkinson officials denied that pressure was applied on the architect, despite earlier newspaper articles that had quoted Jackson directing his staff to find ways to cancel their contract.

The airlines were outraged. They believed that Jackson's social goals were costing them both money and lost time in building the midfield terminal. In May of 1975, the midfield expansion was once again officially delayed. Jackson's minority demands created a feeling of hostility and suspicion between the airlines and the mayor that would persist and intensify through the next seven years of his administration.

Meanwhile, the OPEC oil crisis of 1975 cost the airlines considerably with jet fuel increasing from

Left Photo: Courtesy of Ray Leader, Federal Aviation Administration (Retired), Hartsfield-Jackson Atlanta International Airport. Atlanta Municipal Airport (circa 1970's)

Chapter 3 - The History of the Airport

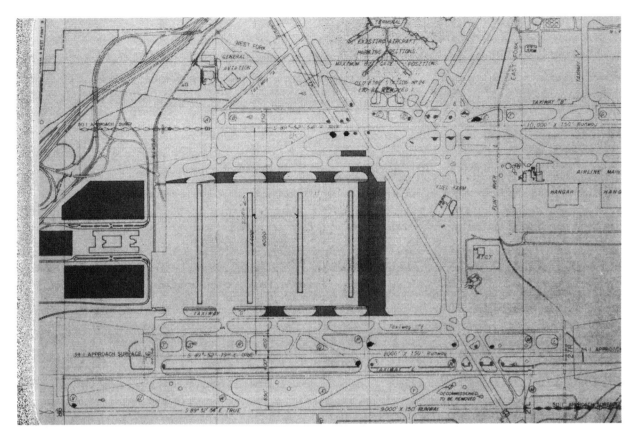

Courtesy of Ray Leader, Federal Aviation Administration (Retired), Hartsfield-Jackson Atlanta International Airport. Initial plans of the 1980 midfield terminal

less then twenty-five cents a gallon to more than a dollar per gallon. This made the delays even more problematic.

there was simply not enough room

The 1961 terminal was persistently overcrowded with over 25 million passengers in 1975 and an estimated 42 million expected by 1980. The gates could handle only eighty-nine aircraft at a time with over a hundred jockeying for space during peak times. Long taxiing times were costing the airlines financially. There was simply not enough room for the aircraft demands.

Meanwhile, Mayor Jackson came under pressure on a number of fronts. The press was severely criticizing him for his minority demands delaying a vital and timely project. Even the black community was irritated because construction workers were waiting to begin and the airport construction would greatly help Atlanta's high unemployment rate, many of whom were black.

The U. S. attorney's office was investigating allegations of unjustified pressure and influence regarding joint ventures. The Fulton County grand jury was urging city council to reject an airport services custodial contract that had gone to the fourth lowest bidder. A state legislative committee had been formed to possibly remove the airport from Atlanta's control and put it into a state airport authority. Governor George Busbee and House Speaker Tom Murphy pledged support for the efforts saying that the delays from the present administration would cause the airport to lose business and adversely effect the state's economy.

Mayor Jackson finally had to face facts. He was the one who had slowed the airport expansion, and it was hurting him politically. Jackson said in an October issue of *The Atlanta Journal and The Atlanta Constitution* that he did not want to be remembered as the man who didn't get the airport built.

Having made his point, Jackson reduced the 25 percent requirement to a "goal" of 20 to 25 percent minority involvement. His other insistence that the minority partners be local, put the white owned contractors in a bind because there were very few black owned firms that met the unique qualifications needed for the airport construction.

this was the design that would have been used

The mid field terminal was originally designed between 1967 and 1969 as a series of mini terminals with parking available right up at the gates. By 1973, the airport had veered away from the drive up to the plane idea, which freed up additional space. Because baggage and ticketing facilities no longer were planned for each mini terminal, more aircraft gates could be added. The people mover train was above ground. This was the design that would have been used had not Mayor Jackson halted the timetable with his minority participation plans in the first half of 1975.

In the winter of 1975, an ice storm at Dallas-Fort Worth caused the international airport to be paralyzed because the above ground transportation system was completely shut down for several days. This ground level people mover was the model for Atlanta's plan. This caused the designer and the airlines quite some anguish. Eventually, the Atlanta

Courtesy of Ray Leader, Federal Aviation Administration (Retired), Hartsfield-Jackson Atlanta International Airport. (circa 1970's)

Chapter 3 - The History of the Airport

plans were changed to an underground train people mover. The airlines were not willing to take a chance of a shut down of the airport because of weather related issues.

By putting the people mover underground, a costly taxiway bridge that separated the north and south runways could be eliminated. The taxiways in earlier layouts that separated ground transportation from air transportation could be eliminated. This move would add an additional twelve gates. These changes created financial savings and decreased the number of concourses needed from five and a half to four. Now, concourses could be constructed east to west instead of the originally planned north to south.

The airlines did demand a back up system to the people mover in the underground transportation mall. They would also build a moving sidewalk which would become the largest in the world and move more people per year than Atlanta's MARTA rail system.

The sheer size of the project was a challenge, according to Tom Ramsey, the chief designer with the Stevens and Wilkinson architectural firm. Ramsey stated that the concourses would be deceptively simple. Officials made a last minute decision to incorporate MARTA's rail system into the ground transportation terminal.

the airport should be named the Atlanta Airport

Mayor Jackson brought George Berry into city government to be the director of airport administration and development. Berry's appointment reassured the airlines and the business community

Courtesy of Ray Leader, Federal Aviation Administration (Retired), Hartsfield-Jackson Atlanta International Airport. Eastern Airlines hub at Atlanta Airport. (circa 1970's)

Courtesy of the Atlanta Hartsfield-Jackson International Airport. Air France flight with Atlanta City skyline in background

because he was known and trusted by them. Berry had the task of wrestling with all of the contracts for the construction of the airport. He ensured that the contractors lived up to the minority participation goals. In 1978, he became the third commissioner of aviation for Atlanta's airport. In 2012, I had the opportunity to speak with Berry who told me that the terminal and concourses were like a high rise building laid on its side. He had also known Mayor Hartsfield who had told him that the airport should be named the Atlanta Airport and did not want it to be named for him.

Berry had to deal with multiple organizations from government, including the FAA, to construction related companies and organizations and the airlines. Berry told how he had to walk a thin line as Georgia law gave strong rights to the low bidder on public jobs and he was charged with working with the firms to help meet the minority participation goals. Berry said he had to pre-qualify the bidders to make sure that he kept things within the law while striving to meet Mayor Jackson's goals.

He found that the biggest obstacle to implementing the minority goals was the FAA, who he had to be convinced that they were not arbitrarily excluding any responsible and qualified bidders.

When the construction process was ready to begin, the bids were awarded to The HOH Company, a joint venture company made from three non Georgia firms. HOH would be the contractor for the main terminal. Their low bid was $93,440,000. A Charlotte North Carolina company, J. A. Jones, would build the people mover tunnel at the low bid of $18,643,826. Two local firms, C. W. Matthews and MacDougald-Warren were also awarded bids. C. W. Matthews would build the paved taxi ways and terminal aprons at $15,657,824. MacDougald-Warren bid $759,508 to build access roads and fencing.

The city also received a $9.8 million grant from the U. S. Department of Transportation that helped finance the widening and moving of Interstate 85 to give the airport more land to use.

Courtesy of Ray Leader, Federal Aviation Administration (Retired), Hartsfield-Jackson Atlanta International Airport. The two rotundas opened in 1968 through the early 1980's. The rotunda gave added gate space in a more concentrated area

construction began on the present day midfield terminal

Finally, construction began on the present day midfield terminal in January 1977, under the administration of Mayor Maynard Jackson. After ten years of false starts, lawsuits, design changes and more, the airport expansion was at last underway with a target completion date of January 1, 1981.

When it was all said and done, it was the largest construction project in the south, costing over $500 million. The William B. Hartsfield Atlanta International Airport opened on September 21, 1980, "on-time and below budget."[10] It was a great accomplishment for the Jackson administration. However, there had been much controversy associated with the construction of the new terminal. Most of the controversy was because of the minority contracts that were awarded to multiple construction companies during the construction.

The new terminal was designed to accommodate up to 55 million passengers per year and covered approximately 2.5 million square feet. At the height of the construction approximately 2,000 workers reported to the site each day. The world's largest airport terminal complex was built surrounded by what was then the second busiest airport in the world while it continued with business as usual.

President Jimmy Carter, a Georgia native and lifelong resident, gave a pre-opening speech on September 16, 1981. A few hours later, he officially became the first passenger to depart from the new terminal.

10. Quote from Maynard Jackson, Atlanta Journal-Constitution, 9-21-1980

The move to the new terminal came in the pre-dawn hours of September 21. The last scheduled flight came into the 1961 terminal late on September 20th, and by 12:30 a.m., the two hour move had begun. Sometime before 3 a.m. the new terminal was operational and the place filled with people. It looked as though the terminal had been open for ten years.

the crowning achievement of Jackson's administration

Mayor Jackson became the first passenger to arrive at the new terminal aboard the private plane of Atlanta Falcons owner Rankin Smith. Mayor Jackson spoke of the new terminal complex as "the crowning achievement of his administration."

In December 1984, a 9,000 foot fourth parallel runway was completed and another runway was extended to 11,889 feet the following year.

In May 2001, construction of a 9,000 foot fifth runway began. It was completed at a cost of $1.28 billion and opened on May 27, 2006, and was the first runway added since 1984. I was privileged to be among many Atlanta dignitaries to be the first to take off from the runway on a Delta jet. In the ceremony that preceded it, I was announced as a Hartsfield family member and representative. The runway was called "The Most Important Runway In America." Having five runways now gave the Atlanta Airport the ability to have what is called triple simultaneous departures and arrivals. Atlanta is one of few airports in the world that has this unique ability.

On the south side of the airport, the fifth runway bridges over Interstate 285, the Atlanta perimeter.

Courtesy of Ray Leader, Federal Aviation Administration (Retired), Hartsfield-Jackson Atlanta International Airport. Eastern concourse 1970's

The building of the fifth runway was a massive project, which involved putting fill dirt eleven stories high in some places, destroyed some surrounding neighborhoods and dramatically changed the scenery of two cemeteries on the property. Flat Rock Cemetery and Hart Cemetery had to be relocated. The runway was added to help ease some of the traffic problems caused by landing small and mid size aircraft on the longer runways which are also used by larger planes, such as the Boeing 777. The fifth runway increased the capacity for landings and take offs by 40%, from an average of 184 flights per hour to 237 flights per hour.

Along with the construction of the fifth runway, a new control tower was built so that controllers could see the entire length of the runway. The new control tower is the tallest airport control tower in the United States, with a height of over 398 feet. The old tower, 585 feet away from the new control tower, was demolished on August 5, 2006.

In January 2012, I was allowed by the FAA to take a professional photographer, Bob McGill, of Shutterbug Studios, into the tower to take pictures of the airport. It was a privilege to see the airport from this vantage point because the FAA rarely allows any photography from the tower.

On October 20, 2003, Atlanta's city council voted to change the name from Hartsfield Atlanta International Airport to the current Hartsfield–Jackson Atlanta International Airport. It was to honor the former Mayor Maynard Jackson, the first African-American mayor of Atlanta, who had died on June

Courtesy of the Atlanta Hartsfield-Jackson International Airport. Aerial photo of fifth runway during construction over I-285

Courtesy of the Atlanta Hartsfield-Jackson International Airport. Aerial photo of fifth runway during construction

23, 2003. The council had initially planned on renaming the airport solely for Mayor Jackson, but public outcry, especially by Mayor Hartsfield's descendants, prompted the compromise. In a following chapter, called 2003, I explain this further.

The Taxiway Victor, an "end-around taxiway" opened in April 2007. It saves an estimated $26 to $30 million a year in fuel costs by allowing airplanes on the north runways to taxi to the gate. The taxiway drops some 30 feet from the runway elevation which allows other aircraft to take off and land simultaneously.

As a result of the drought in 2007, the airport (the eighth-largest water user in the state) has made changes to reduce water usage. The changes include making adjustments to 725 toilets, 338 urinals and 601 sinks. The two terminal buildings alone use and average of 917,000 gallons or about 3.5 million liters each day. The airport suspended the practice of using fire trucks to spray water over an aircraft, known as a water salute, when a pilot makes a last landing before retirement. The airport today employs approximately 55,300 employees, including airline, ground transportation, concessionaire, security, federal government, and City of Atlanta and airport tenant employees. It is considered the largest employer in the State of Georgia. With a payroll of $2.4 billion, the airport has a direct and indirect economic impact of $3.2 billion on the local and regional economy, and a total annual regional economic impact of more than $19.8 billion. [11]

11. www.Atlanta-Airport.com

Courtesy of Bob McGill © 2012 Shutterbug Studios. The taxiway victor in the background drops thirty feet allowing planes to taxi around during multiple arrivals and departures

In my 2009 interview with Mayor Sam Massell, he told me how Hartsfield got the airport into the city limits. As the airport continued to grow and expand, Hartsfield knew that it needed to be in the city limits. The annexation had to be continuous. The airport property was separated by portions of Hapeville and East Point. Hartsfield then annexed the highway (now Interstate 75/85) and added the airport property into the City of Atlanta.

Mayor Massell said that Hartsfield "was proud" of the airport. He knew how to make money for the airport. One of the ways was the observation deck that he had built so private individuals could go and watch the planes take off and land. Hartsfield did not profit personally from the observation deck. The funds collected were used for the expansion and renovation of the 1946 terminal.

Courtesy of Georgia State University Magazine. Photographer Ben Rollins. Mayor Sam Massell in 2014

Courtesy of Ray Leader, Federal Aviation Administration (Retired), Hartsfield-Jackson Atlanta International Airport. Delta concourse 1970's

Courtesy of Ray Leader, Federal Aviation Administratio (Retired), Hartsfield-Jackson Atlanta International Airport. Terminal early 1970's

Chapter 3 - The History of the Airport

Courtesy of Ray Leader, Federal Aviation Administration (Retired), Hartsfield-Jackson Atlanta International Airport. Rotunda 1968 through 1981

Courtesy of Ray Leader, Federal Aviation Administration (Retired), Hartsfield-Jackson Atlanta International Airport. Delta 747 and Deltla DC-9

Courtesy of Ray Leader, Federal Aviation Administration (Retired), Hartsfield-Jackson Atlanta International Airport. Aerial view of terminal 1970's

Courtesy of Ray Leader, Federal Aviation Administration (Retired), Hartsfield-Jackson Atlanta International Airport. British Airways Concorde 1970's

Courtesy of the Atlanta Hartsfield-Jackson International Airport. Midfield terminal construction, late 1970's

Courtesy of Ray Leader, Federal Aviation Administration (Retired), Hartsfield-Jackson Atlanta International Airport. Delta flight 1979

Courtesy of Ray Leader, Federal Aviation Administration (Retired), Hartsfield-Jackson Atlanta International Airport

Courtesy of Ray Leader, Federal Aviation Administration (Retired), Hartsfield-Jackson Atlanta International Airport

Courtesy of Ray Leader, Federal Aviation Administration (Retired), Hartsfield-Jackson Atlanta International Airport

Courtesy of Ray Leader, Federal Aviation Administration (Retired), Hartsfield-Jackson Atlanta International Airport

Chapter Four
Atlanta has a History of Changing Names

Atlanta, as it is known today, has had several previous names that most Atlantans would not recognize. Officially and unofficially, the names have included the following: Deanville, Thrasherville, Terminus, Marthasville, Standing Peachtree, Canebreak (or Canebrake), Whitehall, and currently Atlanta. Hopefully, in the future, the City of Atlanta government officials will not consider changing the Atlanta name again.

One of the first names for Atlanta was a fort named "Standing Peachtree." Lt. George Gilmer, a future Georgia governor, gave the fort that name. It is believed to have been the name of an old Indian village in the area. Early settlers called the area Canebreak or Canebrake, spelled differently in different sources. On June 9, 1835, the federal government recognized the area as "Whitehall" because of the naming of the Whitehall Post Office.

Colonel Abbott Hall Brisbane, the Chief Engineer of the W&A Railroad, named the area Terminus in September of 1837. The name Terminus was never an official name.

Between 1837 and 1842, the area was called Deanville, after Lemuel Dean who claimed at that time to have owned the property. During those years, it was also called Thrasherville, after John J. Thrasher. He was an entrepreneur, a railroad builder, a merchant, and a politician, who physically and economically laid the foundations of what would become modern day Atlanta. Affectionately known as "Cousin John" by friends and strangers, he has been called one of Georgia's most colorful historical figures. His 1839 railroad settlement, known as "Thrasherville", went through a few changes before it officially became Atlanta in 1845.

General William T. Sherman and the Union Army ransacked Thrasher's elegant Ashby Street home during Sherman's march on Atlanta in 1864 but

Courtesy of Bob MGill, 2012, Shutterbug Atlanta. Atlanta skyline

it remained as a residence to some of the city's most prominent families until 1931. Thrasher was a speculator by nature who made and lost several small fortunes according to Atlanta historian Franklin M. Garrett in his book, ***Atlanta and Environs: A Chronicle of Its People and Events***.

J. Edgar Thomson, Chief Engineer of the Georgia Railroad, was responsible for naming the city Atlanta in 1845. Mr. Thomson gave varying stories about how he came up with the name, but my personal favorite is that the city was named for former Governor Wilson Lumpkin's daughter. Her middle name was Atalanta (spelling included an "a" as the third letter) after the fleet-footed goddess from Roman mythology. Between 1843 and 1845, the city was also called Marthasville for Governor Lumpkin's daughter whose first name was Martha.[1] This trend of name changing continues throughout the course of Atlanta's history.

1. www.ngeorgia.com

upcoming name change at the airport

On July 6, 2003, an article by D. L. Bennett in the ***Atlanta Journal-Constitution*** entitled "New Faces & Old Places," begins to tell the story of the upcoming name change at the airport. More importantly it showed how Atlanta does not have a sense of history and has a questionable habit of changing the names of things.

Mr. Bennett wrote about changing names of several old places, streets and buildings in Atlanta. He noted that all one had to do was to walk along Peachtree Street to see the city's many new buildings that were the third or fourth replacements for the original structures of which many had new names. Bennett noted that more than forty Atlanta streets had changed names in the past twenty years.

Courtesy of Bob McGill © 2012 Shutterbug Atlanta. Atlanta skyline from the FAA control tower

Courtesy of Hartsfield-Jackson Atlanta International Airport (circa 1990's)

Thirty parks and other city buildings also were given new names. The school system had also changed names of their public places on a regular basis. Bennett wrote the article because he foresaw the possibility of the upcoming name change at the airport following Mayor Jackson's death.

Bennett also interviewed area history buff Anne Boutwell who noted that these changes had created turmoil that was "disconcerting" to say the least. She said Atlanta needed to remember and honor its founding fathers even if they look out of step with modern times. "I have a passion for history" Ms. Boutwell said. If you change an area's history then you are changing the history of it's people and you may loose a sense of the area's identity. She noted that "Atlanta has lost its identity many times."

Bennett said civil war era names such as Beauregard, Jeptha, Stewart and Confederate had all been replaced in the past twenty years. New honors had been put into place for John Wesley Dobbs, Andrew Young, Martin Luther King Jr., Benjamin Bickers, Joseph Lowery, Jesse Hill, Hosea Williams, and Ralph David Abernathy, who were all civil rights and community leaders of a more recent history. [2]

"That's the city re-creating itself," said Council woman Carla Smith. "We care about history but we keep choosing to change it." In 2002, the Atlanta City Council became concerned about how the city kept changing the name of streets, parks and buildings so the city appointed a committee headed by Smith to look into ways of keeping our history. The council eventually recommended adopting a process much like a rezoning for name changes adding that they wanted more community input.

Mayor Shirley Franklin put into place the Atlanta Advisory Committee in July 2003 with the purpose of finding ways to honor Mayor Jackson and Mayor Allen. In 2002, Councilwoman Smith's committee had recommended the use of honorary signs on intersections, planters, benches or other

2. AJC by D. L. Bennett, 7-6-2003, p. E1

*Courtesy of Hartsfield-Jackson Atlanta International Airport.
1961 Terminal of Atlanta Municipal Airport*

monuments instead of constantly changing street names. "We need to look at what we are doing." Smith said we are taking away things that may have historical significance. "Is our history important?" Ah! That is the same question the Hartsfield family and I had asked early on in the discussions with city officials when they started talking about changing the airport name.

but in 2003 they did it again

In 2002, the city looked at how they had a habit of changing names and vowed to do something about it which should have stopped flippant name changes. But in 2003, they did it again! This time, it was probably the biggest name change of them all. It wasn't a street or a building, it was the busiest airport in the world. Are you kidding me?

Over the years in some cases, Atlanta replaced the name of a prominent figure who was once honored yet that person quietly slipped into history because there were no longer close relatives left to speak for them. An example was Benjamin T. Hunter, the state's first school commissioner, who once had a street named for him. Today that street bears the name of Martin Luther King, Jr. Hartsfield International almost fell into that category. Although I was a distant Hartsfield relative of which there were few close relatives, I felt that the airport should remain named for Mayor Hartsfield. For thirty two years it was called William B. Hartsfield Atlanta International Airport in his honor. Other members of the family and I diligently fought to retain this honor.

Bennett started his column in July with the following: "Doug Dean is ready to rewrite Atlanta history. Hartsfield who? He says." Doug Dean, an Atlanta state representative, said the city can't be afraid to consign one time heroes to footnotes in old history books. New Atlanta should honor today's heroes according to Dean. So I would ask, will we change it again for tomorrow's heroes? Dean wanted the city to remove the name of William Berry Hartsfield from the Atlanta airport and replace it with Maynard Holbrook Jackson, Jr. Or simply trade the name of one old mayor for a more recent one. "His time has passed," Dean said of Hartsfield. Sometimes you have to change the names of the past to honor those who have worked hard to make advances for the current generation. Hartsfield is part of the past and my kids and your kids need to know about the contributions of Maynard Jackson.

Dean's comments were unsettling. The change that was being considered at the airport was one that has played out in Atlanta for more than two decades as a new generation of Atlanta leaders had set out to honor their heroes. The rush to create civic monuments for recent heroes has reduced our once well known residents to long forgotten black and white pictures and footnotes in history books.

Mayor Hartsfield's name dropped or hyphenated

To me comments like those of Doug Dean are heartbreaking. I don't understand why he felt that it was necessary to replace Mayor Hartsfield's name at the airport. In 2003 interviews, I stated that Mayor Maynard Jackson should be honored but I did not want to see Mayor Hartsfield's name dropped or hyphenated. Some called me racist for saying that, but I believe changing the name was somewhat racial. To keep the name Hartsfield was out of respect for one who had already been deservedly honored. I believe Mr. Dean was part of the problem with government officials. Although he was not a city official, making those kind of statements as a state official were very unfortunate.

This quote also appeared in the Bennett column. "This is a trend that's been going on for a while," said Andy Ambrose, Deputy Director of the Atlanta History Center. "It's not surprising, because Atlanta's been so focused on the future. There's not been that reverence for the past you find in other cities."

Atlanta has been known to make some good name changes along the way. I know I have said that they had a bad habit of changing names but the following changes should have been made because they were the right thing to do. For example, Nathan Bedford Forrest once had a couple of streets and parks

Courtesy of Hartsfield-Jackson Atlanta International Airport. Downtown Atlanta 2000

named for him. He was a Confederate general and the first leader of the Ku Klux Klan. He should not have been honored because of his association with this hateful organization.

In 2003 Bennett also interviewed Cathy Loving, a historian, who kept up with school system history in an archive and museum that she maintained. She kept running tallies on name changes as well as files on everyone who was so honored, even if their name later got replaced. As a historian, she found all the name changes in Atlanta disconcerting. "You can't wash the history away"' Loving said.

Bennett interviewed me by phone for his article. I told him that I did not think it was right to rename things and that I would hate to see the airport renamed. It was the first of many times that I was quoted in the *Atlanta Journal-Contitution*.

Anne Boutwell, the history buff that said Atlanta had lost its identity many times, also said that she did not see an end to Atlanta changing names and perceived history.

at least forty streets in Atlanta today have changed names

According to Jolomo.net, there are at least forty streets in Atlanta today that have changed names over the years, some more than once. Antebellum gristmills and sawmills left behind traces through such names as Moore's Mill Road and Howell Mill Road.

Many of Atlanta's more famous streets were once called something else including: Auburn Avenue, Boulevard, Broad Street, Capital Avenue, Carnegie Way, Centennial Olympic Park Boulevard, Courtland Street, Edgewood, Georgia Avenue, Glen Iris Drive, Martin Luther King Jr. Drive, Memorial Drive, Metropolitan Pkwy, Northside Drive, Piedmont Avenue and Park Place (for Woodruff Park). Peachtree Center Avenue replaced Ivy Street (for Hardy Ivy, the first Atlanta settler). Peachtree Street replaced Whitehall Street, one of Atlanta's oldest streets dating back to the Civil War.

The previous names are not a complete list. Do Atlanta government officials care about preserving Atlanta's history? They have been changing the names of streets, buildings, parks, and even the airport for a long time. Remember the Atlanta airport has had five official names.

Here is a pretty interesting side note that I discovered in my research. There are 71 streets with the word "Peachtree" in them in the metro Atlanta area. This official count comes from the Atlanta Regional Commission.

Not only does the city itself change names, it seems that many organizations and businesses do so as well. A Baptist college moved to Atlanta in 1878 and went through several name changes before it eventually became Morehouse College.

Delta Air Lines was once Delta Air Corporation. Eastern Air Lines was formed from a composite of assorted air travel corporations, including Florida Air Ways and Pitcairn Aviation. Air Tran Airways started as ValuJet and is now Southwest Airlines.

Another famous airport went through a name change in 1998. Washington National became Ronald Reagan Washington National Airport.

even the historical society changed its name

The Atlanta Historical Society changed its name to the Atlanta History Center in 1990. So, what can we expect from the city if even the historical society has changed its name. The City of Atlanta is not the only institution that has regularly changed the names of things. Many other cities, states, businesses, and organizations have done the same. However, Atlanta does have one of the worst records for changing names. What purpose does it serve to continue to change names? I personally don't understand because it is confusing, costly, and time consuming.

In 1974, the Fox Theatre became an endangered property. Atlanta's largest and grandest theater was scheduled to become a new high-rise corporate headquarters. This plan would have probably included a name change and complete destruction of a famous Atlanta landmark.

A grass-roots campaign to "Save the Fox" quickly emerged. It was uncharacteristic for Atlanta. The campaign included a group of local high school students who picketed in front of the theatre gaining critical media attention. Aided by then Mayor Maynard Jackson, the city's Urban Design

Courtesy of Dale Hartsfield, 2014, Woodruff Arts Center on Peachtree Street, Atlanta, Georgia. Robert Woodruff, former CEO of Coca Cola, was a lifelong friend of William B. Hartsfield

Commission, and Atlanta Landmarks, Inc., a new non-profit organization, the campaign succeeded. This movement to save the Fox brought the City together which was good for Atlanta.

In 1975, The Urban Design Commission, with grants from the State Historic Preservation Office, conducted the city's first survey of historic resources and began the city's first historic preservation ordinances. The Atlanta Preservation Center, a private, non-profit association founded in 1980, assisted the Commission. A new

Courtesy of Dale Hartsfield, 2014, Fox Theatre, Atlanta, Georgia

comprehensive historic preservation ordinance in 1989 gave the city the tools it needed to preserve what remained of the city's architectural heritage. In addition to more than one hundred and thirty National Register properties, the city now has more than fifty landmark buildings and a dozen historic districts. According to an essay by Tommy Jones, an Architectural Historian with the National Park Service's Southeast Regional Office, these are now protected by local ordinances.

The Fox Theatre was designated a National Historic Landmark in 1976.

change names again? Probably!

I would hope one day we will name something of importance and leave it's name in tact forever. We now have in place historical societies and a national park organization that's sole purpose is to maintain an organization's name and historical accounts. Again we must ask, is our history important? Will the airport as well as other streets and buildings change names again? Unfortunately, probably so.

I am reminded of the cartoon that Mike Luckovich, editorial cartoonist of the **Atlanta Journal-Contitution**, did in the late summer of 2003. The punch line was: "Welcome To Numerous Dead Mayors of Atlanta International Airport."

The Vent, a section in the **Atlanta Journal-Constitution**, is designed for readers to write in and "vent" or complain about a particular issue they

"By permission of Mike Luckovich and Creators Syndicate, Inc." Political cartoons in the Atlanta Journal Constitution created by Mike Luckovich

Chapter 4 - Atlanta has a History of Changing Names

have read in the *AJC*. Some of the vents concerning the renaming of the airport were priceless.

One of my favorites said:

"Next time Atlanta wants to honor someone, it should rename Punce Dah Lee-ahan (Ponce De Leon) Avenue. After all, nobody in this city can pronounce that Spanish guy's name, and he's been dead even longer than Mayor Hartsfield."

Another vent said:

"So many great men to honor, so few unnamed airports." [3]

I hope you get the point that a lot of people thought the entire renaming thing was ridiculous. I agreed but also thought it was depressing. Sadly, we can expect names to change again. After all, the City of Atlanta and other governments seem to feel the need to honor their most recent heroes and lay aside the memories and contributions of our many former heroes!

I find this disappointing and regrettable because future generations will not get a correct sense of our local and national history as well as our personal connection with it. We can only hope that as a nation we can grasp the importance of our history and try to preserve it's integrity and it's cherished names!

History cannot be changed, but people can alter the discussion of it and how it is written in our history books. The actual facts can be ignored or denied, as it often is.

3. AJC, The Vent, Monday, 11-3-2003

Courtesy of Dale Hartsfield, 2014, One of many famous Atlanta street names

Chapter Five
2003

On June 23, 2003, Atlanta's first African-American Mayor, Maynard H. Jackson, Jr., died unexpectedly on a business trip in Washington, D. C. His death would lead to a significant change in the history of Atlanta's airport. The airport already had a distinguished name that was recognized around the world, William B. Hartsfield Atlanta International Airport. It was also known as the busiest airport in the world.

At the time of Mayor Jackson's death, I was not prepared for the upcoming changes that would occur in my life over the next several months. 2003 became a very significant year for me because of the controversy that would follow these events.

As soon as I heard of Mayor Jackson's passing, I heard Andrew Young, another former Atlanta mayor, speaking on the radio. He eagerly and purposefully stated that he thought the city should name the airport for Mayor Jackson. While I was driving and casually listening to the radio, I heard Andrew Young's comments. I almost drove off the road! Upon hearing that, with what I knew about the airport and it's name, I wondered what in the world could Mayor Jackson have possibly done to deserve an honor such as that.

naming the airport for Jackson was preposterous

When the airport was deservedly named for Mayor Hartsfield, I was in the eighth grade at Briarwood High School in East Point, GA. When I was in the tenth grade, Maynard Jackson was first elected the Mayor of Atlanta. I did not remember what Mayor Jackson had done to deserve having Hartsfield International renamed for him. The airport had grown during Mayor Jackson's tenure in the 1970's

Courtesy of the Hartsfield-Jackson Atlanta International Airport. View of downtown Atlanta

Chapter 5 - 2003

129

Courtesy of Bob McGill © 2012 Shutterbug Atlanta. View of runways and concoures from the FAA control tower

and 1980's, but naming the airport for Jackson was preposterous.

I heard this "idea" thrown around several times before it was suppressed for a short period. Mayor Shirley Franklin, Atlanta's then serving mayor, said she and the Atlanta City Council were going to name an independent panel. Together, they would decide how the city would honor Mayor Jackson, as well as Mayor Ivan Allen, another former mayor who also died in the summer of 2003.

I have often ask what was the reason for the 2003 name change. Was it about honor, politics, race, or something else? Perhaps it was a combination of several, but to me, it was not a credible reason.

"The Commission (called the Atlanta Advisory Commission) - eight African American members, eight Caucasian members, and one member of Asian heritage is made up of nine men and eight women of diverse backgrounds, perspectives, and areas of expertise." [1]

Even the commission was riddled with race overtones regarding the name change. The fight had begun even before the panel (or commission) was ever announced. People began writing to the **Atlanta Journal-Constitution**. Several letters to the editor had been printed, supporting renaming the airport, and several more denouncing such an idea. Obviously, the entire discussion and subject findings did consist of racial aspects and strong opinions. I do not consider myself a racist or bigot. Nonetheless, the discussion to rename the airport had a lot to do with race. The people who participated went pretty much down the line according to their race.

Pete Correll and Jesse Hill were named as co-chairmen of the Commission. Mr. Correll is white and Mr. Hill is black. Included on the commission were: Sallie Adams Daniel, Marie Dodd, Julia Emmons, Sherry Frank, Joan Garner, Ingrid Saunders Jones, Joyce Shepherd, Lani Wong, Rev. Gerald Durley, Bill Fuller, George Goodwin, Bill Ide, Leo Mullen, Lovett Stovall, and Carl Ware. [2]

Mayor Franklin announced that there would be two separate public meetings for Atlanta area residents. They would be allowed to come and discuss their thoughts on how to honor Mayor Jackson and Mayor Allen. The first meeting was held on July 29, 2003. I was unable to attend that first meeting because of a previously scheduled trip to Alaska.

---

1. Atlanta Advisory Commission Final Report, Page 11

2. Atlanta Advisory Commission Final Report, Appendix 1

According to the Atlanta Advisory Committee's final report, "The session was attended by approximately one hundred people, most of whom were African American." Some twenty five individuals spoke publicly at this session. "In addition to personal testimonials, the Commission heard from representatives of the United Youth Adult Conference, who informed the Commission of a petition in support of renaming the airport for Mayor Jackson." There were only a few who addressed how to Honor Mayor Allen. "Broadcast and print media coverage was very heavy for this event." [3]

I knew that I really needed to be there

The second public meeting was held on August 26, 2003. All of this was taking place only two months after the passing of Mayor Jackson. When this meeting was scheduled, there was no doubt that I

3. Atlanta Advisory Commission Final Report, Page 13

would be there to voice my opinion, to not make any changes to the airport name. The airport was already rightfully named for William B. Hartsfield, who was the "father of aviation" in Atlanta, thus William B. Hartsfield Atlanta International Airport.

When I arrived at City Hall that evening, city employees at the entrance were asking people to sign in at the front desk if you desired to speak at the meeting. Approximately thirty five signed up to speak, including Mayor Jackson's widow, Valerie Jackson. I signed up to have my opinion verbalized publicly with my allotted two minutes along with others. I don't remember where I was in the order of speakers, but it was toward the end of the list. When it was my turn to speak, it was running about twenty five to one in favor of naming the airport Jackson International. Only one person had mentioned honoring Mayor Allen. One other elderly white man mentioned Mayor Hartsfield. He said that he knew him and stated firmly that the

Courtesy of Bob McGill © 2012 Shutterbug Atlanta. Controllers in the FAA Atlanta tower

ATLANTA
ADVISORY
COMMISSION

FINAL REPORT

September 19, 2003

HONORING THE LEGACIES OF
MAYORS IVAN ALLEN, JR. AND MAYNARD JACKSON, JR.

Established by Mayor Shirley Franklin and the Atlanta City Council

Courtesy of Dale Hartsfield. Dale's copy of Atlanta Advisory Commission Final Report received due to his involvement in the 2003 name change of the Atlanta Airport

airport should remain Hartsfield International. I regret not having an opportunity to speak with that gentleman after the meeting. Unfortunately, I did not get his name as I was in deep thought about what I had to say during my two minutes.

Hartsfield like the airport

When it was my turn to speak, I introduced myself as Dale Hartsfield, "Hartsfield, like the airport." When they heard my name, the room filled with a gasp followed by complete silence. Suddenly, I felt a little intimidated. Most of the people in the audience were African-American. Although I do not judge people by the color of their skin, I was one of very few white people in the crowd. Intimidated or not, I had always tried to stand up for my beliefs and principals. I was the only person named Hartsfield who spoke at either of the public forums. No other Hartsfield family member was present. It seemed strange that no other member of the Hartsfield family was present. The closest living relatives of Mayor Hartsfield either lived out of town or were in poor health. Even though I was not a kissing cousin, I had strong feelings about the airport name of Hartsfield International and did not want to see it changed.

When my turn came to speak, I explained to the crowd that the airport was already properly named for the man who worked tirelessly to develop the airport from it's humble beginnings, and I strongly believed that the airport should remain Hartsfield International. After I finished my speech, a few more spoke about Mayor Jackson, and then the moderator closed the meeting.

At the close of the meeting, reporters surrounded me immediately. Questions were flying, bright lights were on, cameras were rolling and microphones were in my face. I was somewhat stunned and overwhelmed. There must have been twenty five or more reporters, and they all wanted to talk to me. It was apparent this was going to be a big story and it was. With the name Hartsfield, the focus was on me. Over the next couple of months, it became a huge story in Atlanta, some said too big.

Dick Yarbrough, a syndicated columnist, wrote an article that was published in several state newspapers:

Today, the capital city of the Great State of Georgia couldn't manage a two-car funeral. The city is broke and everything in town is broken. Leadership is a scarce commodity. Atlanta is composed of black demagogues, a timid business community and a newspaper that seems powerless to foster positive change. The city that prides itself as "Being Too Busy to Hate" seems to have found ample time to be hateful.

The biggest issue in our dysfunctional capital city these days is not its crumbling sewer system or the pushy panhandlers who act like they own the place. It is renaming Hartsfield International Airport. There is a move on among black politicians to name the airport for former Mayor Maynard Jackson, who died this past July. Jackson was black, or to be politically correct, African-American. Currently, the airport honors former Mayor William B. Hartsfield who was white, or to be politically correct, Caucasian-American. . .

I hope the blacks get their way and ram the name change down everybody's throat. Then in 50 years when Timothy McDonald is in heaven trying to figure out why he's sharing space with white folks and "Able" Mable is trying to get her jaw in neutral, the Hispanic majority in Atlanta will adopt the same strong-arm tactics and change the name of Jackson International to the Cisco Kid International Space Port. [4]

---

4. Excerpts from www.DickYarbrough.com, August 10, 2003

Courtesy of Dale Hartsfield. Escalators from transportation mall to terminal

since it was named for Mayor Hartsfield

Initially, I went to the meeting because I am a Hartsfield and have been introducing myself as Hartsfield like the airport since it was named for Mayor Hartsfield in 1971. Some might view that as a selfish reason and maybe it was. I had hoped that others in the family closer to the Mayor would attend the meetings. Since they were not present, I am very glad that I attended and had the opportunity to express my views. I believe that if I had not been present at that meeting, the airport name would have been changed to Jackson International. From 1971 to 2003, the airport was officially called William B. Hartsfield Atlanta International Airport. I will always believe that name should have remained and never been changed.

I expected to see reporters at the meeting, but clearly was not expecting them to zoom in on me. I became the center of attention that evening and over the next couple of months. As I left city hall, I began to see the influential power of the media in America. When I arrived home, I saw myself on the 10 o'clock news on WAGA channel 5. It was their lead story. At 11:00 pm, Channel 11, WXIA, and Channel 2, WSB, also ran the story of the public meeting early in their newscasts. Excerpts from my speech and interviews with reporters were prominent in each and every news story.

Fame comes and goes, but for a short time, I was the hot topic. Over the next several months, I was interviewed by approximately fifty different reporters, some multiple times. I handed out business cards to a few reporters who requested additional interviews with me in the near future. Reporters often share information with other reporters, otherwise, I would not have received some of the calls I did. The most interesting call I received was from ***The London Financial Times,*** in London, England. I questioned the female reporter about the significance of this story in London. She said with the Atlanta airport being international and the busiest in the world, it definitely was a financial issue that could possibly effect global markets.

taking on city hall is difficult

It was an exciting and adventurous time in my life. It was also a stressful battle, not with reporters, but with City Hall. Taking on City Hall is difficult and may sometimes seem impossible, but worth the fight. As Americans, it is our civil duty and right to question our government officials when they have made decisions on issues that effect our lives as citizens.

Mayor Franklin and other politicians on the city council were adamant about renaming the airport for Mayor Jackson. The idea of hyphenating the name soon surfaced. Once that story was out, I heard that Valerie Jackson, Mayor Jackson's widow, was in agreement with the idea.

Against our family's wishes, Mayor Franklin's appointed commission was proposing to hyphenate and rename the airport Hartsfield-Jackson. After the vote to change the name, a copy of the Atlanta Advisory Commission final report was mailed to my home. On page 22 of the report, it stated that Mrs. Maynard (Valerie) Jackson had met with the commission co-chairs. She had advised that she and the Jackson family would be honored to have the airport renamed Hartsfield-Jackson. The commission had not been respectful enough to discuss this with me or any other members of our family. In fairness to the commission, I realize that

Courtesy of Dale Hartsfield. Arriving airplane at the gate 2012

their purpose was not about Hartsfield but about finding ways to honor Mayor Allen and Mayor Jackson.

hated the idea of the airport name changing

Two days after the public meeting on August 26th, 2003, I received a letter at my home asking if I was the one who had spoke at the public forum. The letter was from Alice Hughes, who said she was a distant relative of Mayor Hartsfield. I did not know her at the time. Alice's mom had been a Hartsfield. Alice, who was a historian, hated the idea of the airport name changing in any possible way. Alice became my greatest supporter in the fight to save the name of the airport. She introduced me to Monty Cheshire, Mayor Hartsfield's grandson. I knew of him, but had never met Monty. Since then, he has become a tremendous help for me in writing this book.

As earlier mentioned, several letters had been written to the *Atlanta Journal-Constitution*. One of these letters was written by Alice Hughes and was published just four days after Mayor Jackson had died.

Alice was already fuming at the thought of renaming Hartsfield. Alice wrote:

> *Plain and simple, William Berry Hartsfield fathered aviation in Atlanta. It is thus appropriate that the airport bears his name. Maynard Jackson certainly deserves to have his name attached to something significant, but why negate the accomplishments of Hartsfield, who brought the City of Atlanta into national prominence? I believe that history is a continuing process to be added to rather than replaced. Why could not City Hall be renamed Jackson City Hall? Also, how about Jackson Centennial Olympic Park? The park is known around the world, and it could well honor the person so largely responsible for bringing the Olympics to Atlanta in 1996.* [5]

Marsha Hartsfield Hendricks, my older sister, had begun making a scrapbook of the articles about the fight from the newspaper accounts. The first time I was quoted was on July 6th. I was quoted often after the meeting on August 26th in the *Atlanta Journal-Constitution.*

Courtesy of the Atlanta Hartsfield-Jackson International Airport. Original midfield tower

5. AJC letter to the editor, 6-27-03

Courtesy of Bob McGill © 2012 Shutterbug Atlanta. The world's busiest airport during a peak time

he did not believe that the city would rename the airport

Once this became public, I began meeting with members of the Hartsfield family, many I had never met. I spoke with Monty at length on several occasions. He expressed to me that he did not believe that the city would rename the airport given the history behind it. I told him that I believed that they would, and if we did not fight that the Hartsfield name was going to be dropped from the airport altogether.

Monty, who lives in Macon, Georgia, did not travel to Atlanta during the next couple of months, even though I tried to get him here. He did write an amazing letter to the City Council, and speak to several members by phone. Monty's letter to the city council appears below:

Honoring Mr. Maynard Jackson
By Monty Cheshire, grandson of past Mayor, William B. Hartsfield

I beg your patience in reading my lengthy comments, so few persons are alive today who remember Mr. Hartsfield personally. I would like to offer a small glimpse into the personality of my grandfather, William B. Hartsfield, in the hope that it may give insight into the dreams of he and Mr. Maynard Jackson. I think great men and women impatiently endure the present while they relentlessly pull the world into their vision for the future. These men, and others, have generously given themselves to the great City of Atlanta.

Memory flashes of my grandfather, William Berry Hartsfield, would include riding around The City in the back of the black Ford city car and being told of developments and projects that an eight year old hardly could appreciate. All he talked of was The City, always. The weekends we, (my parents and I from Macon) would spend in Atlanta visiting my grandparents would always include an unplanned education on the running of The City.

I remember my grandfather sitting at the breakfast table, writing the same sentence

Courtesy of Bob McGill © 2012 Shutterbug Atlanta

with both hands at the same time, and other times, expounding repeatedly that Atlanta was a City with no natural boundaries; that Atlanta could become the largest City in the world. "Why," he would say, "Atlanta could swallow the little towns like Gainesville and Covington and maybe even Macon." William B. Hartsfield was ALL about his love and passion for the City, twenty four seven.

As I grew older, I remember that he seemed to be sought after to speak to groups of mayors from all over the country. In the 50's he was elected to be President of the American Municipal Association of the United States, making him a mayor's Mayor. I remember "Atlanta, the city too busy to hate." Amid such powerful times, his vision was centered on the "final outcome, the world beyond the present strife" and he was busy laying the foundation of cooperation and prosperity for The City as a world player.

Hartsfield's early years as Mayor seemed to be focused on making Atlanta stand out as the logical center for the South, the center for commerce, culture and growth. He traveled around the world consulting domestic and foreign leaders and reviewing their problems and solutions. He recognized transportation to be one of the key pieces in the growth puzzle, and his fascination with the airplane was not in the machine of the present but for what it could become and bring to The City. In today's computer lingo, it was Atlanta's link to the world. In my view, the naming of the airport after Hartsfield was not about the municipal facility but about the labeling of the *most visible and public symbol of the city that he had given his life to develop. Surprisingly, it is the only thing named in his honor.*

Similarly, in my view, Mr. Jackson sought to move The City toward a greater good and to open the prosperity of The City to more people. Investing in the foundation of a sound middle economic class is the key to providing the leaders and volunteers of tomorrow. The airport expansion was an opportunity to invest in people and his leadership maximized that opportunity; it wasn't about brick and mortar, but opportunity for small business and the families that owned and worked for those companies. I can't help but think that Mr. Jackson would want to see his efforts continue in the form of economic and cultural growth of the minorities, the expansion of opportunity for all Atlantans and a sense of community and togetherness for all in "The City." I think it is an error and a missed opportunity to simply "hitch Mr. Jackson's name to the cart of another leader."

My feelings concerning the establishment of an honor for Mr. Maynard Jackson focus on the establishment of a living example to the world of Mr. Jackson's interests and passions for the City and the people he represented. This could be expressed in a "Heartbeat of Atlanta Center," unique to the world, an exhibition, instructional and networking forum dedicated to the continued improvement of the quality of life among minorities in Atlanta.

It is my belief that Mr. Jackson would have supported the continuation of his legacy and passion as reflected in the quality of life of minority Atlantan's. These families are now better able to provide for their children, a secure and respectable home, quality schooling and a sense of community all brought about by Mr. Jackson's work to grow better jobs, provide quality leadership and establish good business role models.

Such a center would highlight the building of the city's economy, and provide a center for

Courtesy of Dale Hartsfield

Chapter 5 - 2003

Courtesy Dale Hartsfield. Many military soldiers pass through the Atlanta Airport every day

instruction and inspiration to small business. Persons challenged with low economic prospects could seek guidance, inspiration and net working opportunities through participating business with the center. This proposed center for minorities actively networking for the good of all would serve as a model for cities around the world. That's the kind of city Atlanta is and that's one way Mr. Maynard Jackson would be remembered and his vision preserved.

Monty Cheshire

their minds seemed to be already made up

Monty's letter and ideas were never mentioned in the media. The letter was sent to all of the city council members. I would hope that some of the council members read it, but I do not know. I believe they already had their minds made up and didn't want any outside influence to affect their decision. The majority wanted to make Mayor Jackson's name the sole name on the airport or at least hyphenated, so that Jackson's name would be a part of the busiest airport in the world.

The Atlanta leadership and Mayor Shirley Franklin, gained much of their power and authority while Jackson was in office. To the Hartsfield family, it appeared that their allegiance to Jackson had a strong influence during the renaming decision.

Due to my out spoken nature, I became the Hartsfield family spokesman. I had taken a stand and found myself fighting city hall. The racial tensions had been stirred and were surfacing during this battle. During this time, racial tensions were down played by most everyone, and thankfully, by the media. Fighting City Hall was stressful enough, the racial aspect just added more fuel to the controversy.

It is quite a challenging task to fight City Hall, but it was well worth the effort and time involved. Because I am a Hartsfield and a relative of the late former Mayor, I felt the airport name dispute was worth fighting for. High expectations by friends and family were set, expecting that I stand up for this honorable cause and defend the Hartsfield name.

A friend, Dr. Joe Teal, resident of Dallas, Georgia, had also previously fought with another city hall in Alabama. He wrote a book about his conflict. It is called, ***Fight City Hall and Win: I Did It And So Can You***. Dr. Teal and I have future plans to conduct seminars discussing, "how to fight city hall," because it can be done successfully.

Eddie Williams, another friend who is a professional speaker, is of mixed race both black and white. Eddie Williams and I, have plans to speak on race relations in America. His book entitled, ***Son of a Solder***, deals with growing up as a mixed race individual. [6]

6. www.eddie-williams.com, www.Hartsfieldspeakers.com

Some people expressed they thought we failed in our battle with City Hall. I disagree. I did not want Mayor Jackson's name added to the airport. If I had not engaged in this controversy, I believe the name Hartsfield would have been removed permanently, and that would have been a sad day for Atlanta.

she wanted the airport named for Mayor Jackson

Several members of my family and I met with Mayor Franklin on two separate occasions to discuss this issue. Even though Mayor Franklin was professional and personable, I believe she was firm in her beliefs that she wanted the airport named for Mayor Jackson who was one of her mentors.

Among the members of my family who supported our fight and went to at least one meeting with me at city hall were: Alice Hughes, whose mother was a Hartsfield, my wife Amy, my son Walt, my sister Marsha Hartsfield Hendricks, Charlie Hartsfield, a grand nephew of Mayor Hartsfield and his daughter Joy Hartsfield.

Cynthia Tucker, the **Atlanta Journal-Constitution** Editorial Page Editor, surprised me with two columns that she wrote during the re-naming fight. Tucker, who is black, went against the majority of the African-American leadership in Atlanta by voicing an opinion that supported keeping the airport named for Hartsfield. In her July 2, 2003, column entitled "Put Jackson Aloft, But Not At The Airport," Tucker wrote:

There ought to be a lasting tribute to the man who helped transform Atlanta from second rung burg to new south capital. But Jackson's fans are wrong to push renaming Hartsfield International Airport after him. While his hallmark accomplishment was an affirmative action model that used a huge public works project, construction of a new airport terminal, to create black wealth, he was not the

Courtesy of Bob McGill © 2012 Shutterbug Atlanta

visionary who built an international airport from nothing. That was the late William B. Hartsfield, who deserves to be remembered for it. As it is, Atlanta does to little to preserve its history.

Tucker continued with some ideas about how Mayor Jackson should be honored. Later in the same article she wrote:

Jackson was not a politician so much as an elemental political force, pushing Atlanta to become the great international city it has always claimed to be. That city is already known worldwide for an airport called Hartsfield, a name and a place Jackson was happy to celebrate in life. It seems unlikely that Jackson would have wanted to change the name in his honor.[7]

7. AJC 7-2-2003 p. A-15

Courtesy of the Atlanta Hartsfield-Jackson International Airport. Mayor Shirley Franklin, 2006

AJC readers responded to Tucker's column with letters to the editor. On July 7, 2003, three letters were published on the editorial page.

Gary Johnson of Atlanta responded:

With the passing of civic and political leaders, local governments are quick to change the names of buildings and other civic projects for their newly departed friend.[8]

As he stated, that was exactly what Atlanta leaders were now seeking to do to honor Mayor Jackson. Many times on TV and in other interviews, I stated that Atlanta should honor Mayor Jackson, just not at the airport, which was Tucker's sentiments.

but why take away an honor

Weeks went by while the discussion bounced back and forth, from changing completely to hyphenating the airport name. I continued my stance of leaving the current name untouched. In my October 6, 2003, speech to the Atlanta City Council, I said, "The Hartsfield family does not have a problem honoring Mayor Jackson. We agreed that Atlanta should honor him, but why take away an honor that was bestowed on Mayor Hartsfield."

Richard K. Collins, of Columbus, Ohio, wrote to the editor in a letter titled "Times Change: So Should Names." He wrote:

I respect her concern for keeping historical ties. However, times are changing. As grand as the Atlanta airport is, and considering Jackson's grand way of doing business, why not?"[9]

8. AJC Editorial Page, Readers Respond
9. AJC Editorial Page, Readers Respond

Courtesy of Dale Hartsfield. Arriving American passenger flight

If Mr. Collins really respected historical ties, why would he support changing the name of an airport that has carried the name for thirty two years? It was named for William B. Hartsfield, who was the "father of aviation" in Atlanta.

About a month into the debate, I received a call from Larry Copeland, a reporter for the *USA Today* newspaper. I was astonished to realize this story had circulated like wildfire across the country. The article included my quotes taken from the Atlanta paper, Atlanta radio and TV.

Mr. Copeland wrote an exceptional and informative article. It included history of the airport as well as highlights of both Mayor Hartsfield and Mayor Jackson's accomplishments.

airport renaming splits Atlantans

The headline in the *USA Today* read "Airport Renaming Splits Atlantans," with a sub title of "Supporters of two former mayor's debate whose name is most worthy of being on facility." That title seemed to sum up the discussions.

Copeland noted, "Hartsfield's family wants the airport name left alone." Copeland said of the advisory commission appointed by Mayor Franklin:

The panel proposed leaving Hartsfield's name alone on the airport and naming its new one billion dollar international terminal, scheduled to open in 2006, for Jackson. That suited many traditionalists and the Hartsfield family.

Later in the article he said:

On Thursday, Maynard Jackson's widow, Valerie Jackson said she now supports naming the airport for both mayors. [10]

Copeland found the following quote from Walt Hartsfield, my son, in the *AJC* on September 23, 2003.

'It is disrespectful,' Walt Hartsfield, a distant cousin of the city's longest-serving mayor, said of the suggestion to change the airport's name. William Hartsfield, who served for

10. USA Today article by Larry Copeland 10-2-03, p. C-1

most of the years between 1937 and 1962, nurtured the airport to become a regional hub for passenger service.

'How would they feel if they changed it ten years down the road and took both their names off? Walt Hartsfield said. [11]

Copeland also wrote about the racial tension from the debate, which is discussed in the next chapter.

renaming airport would snub history

On August 6, 2003, Cynthia Tucker's headline in her editorial page column said, "Renaming airport would snub history." In the article, she wrote:

But if the airport is renamed, the city will send a message that tribute is fleeting and history is anything but sacred. A Jackson International Airport could easily be renamed 20 or 30 years from now, when another beloved mayor or City Council member or congressman dies and his supporters demand commemoration.

Atlanta has a hard enough time remembering its history as it is. A transportation center that burst into being shortly before the Civil War, Atlanta doesn't have the heritage of New Orleans or Savannah, the culture of Boston or the history of New York City. And what little history the city does have, it disrespects. [12]

A year prior, the Atlanta City Council said they wanted to keep history in tact and stop changing names of civic and public buildings, streets and airports. Was anyone listening?

Grace T. Peterson, of Atlanta, wrote to the editor in response to a July 1st story about Mayor Franklin's Atlanta Advisory Commission panel. The panel was selected to study how to honor Mayor Jackson and Mayor Allen.

Although Maynard Jackson was the mayor of the city during reconstruction of Hartsfield

11. AJC 9-23-2003, P. B1

12. AJC 8-6-2003, P. A11

Courtesy of Bob McGill © 2012 Shutterbug Atlanta. Departing jet from the Delta terminal

Courtesy of Bob McGill © 2012 Shutterbug Atlanta

International Airport, Mayor William B. Hartsfield was responsible for securing and attracting the airports global appeal and use.

As a native Atlantan, I feel very strongly that the airport should remain Hartsfield International Airport. Surely there are other venues that could reflect Jackson's direct influence, maybe something relating to the Olympics. [13]

George Barton, of Sharpsburg, wrote:

Renaming Hartsfield International Airport after anyone else would be a mistake. The airport is world famous. Atlanta and Hartsfield are synonymous, and changing the name would cause international confusion and be detrimental to Atlanta.

Centennial Olympic Park would be a much better memorial for Mayor Maynard Jackson. He helped bring the Olympic Games to Atlanta, A larger-than-life statue of Jackson, with his fabulous smile, could be placed at the entrance, and he could greet visitors to Atlanta forever. [14]

On Monday, July 7, 2003, the following comment was sent to The Vent:

Please don't change Hartsfield's name. When flying home late some night, I don't want to find out a mistake was made on my ticket and the plane is landing in Jackson, Mississippi. [15]

The metro area sentiment seemed to be against renaming the airport. Paul Suggs, of Stone Mountain, said:

It upsets me greatly to see our streets and expressways renamed. I am really opposed to renaming the airport, no matter how much the recent mayors who are deceased contributed

13. AJC Editorial Page, Readers Respond, 7-4-2003
14. AJC Editorial Page, Readers Respond, 7-4-2003
15. AJC Vent, 7-4-2003, p. B2

Chapter 5 - 2003

because that was their job, and we should have expected their efforts. [16]

Maynard Jackson International Airport

However, there were some that wanted to see the airport named for Mayor Jackson. Darryl Dean, of Lithonia, said:

Although Cynthia Tucker's points were well thought out, the fact remains that the current airport remains the biggest legacy Maynard Jackson will be remembered for. Therefore, renaming that airport in his honor is the most logical national recognition to reflect Atlanta's New South leadership.

It is fitting that travelers around the world begin to say "Maynard Jackson International Airport." [17]

Colin Campbell, an *AJC* columnist, wrote a column entitled, "Memorial Guidelines needed in Atlanta." His column began with the ideas about the compromised hyphenated name. Campbell wrote:

The debate over what to name the airport turned sour. So Mayor Shirley Franklin finally switched gears and proposed a compromise, a hyphenated name in black and white: Hartsfield-Jackson. You have to assume the City Council will go along.

The proposed name looks like a mouthful, but we will probably get used to it. Today, people call the airport "Hartsfield" or the "airport" or "the Atlanta airport."

Campbell went on to note that it might have been "wiser" if Mayor Franklin had said what she thought from the beginning and not appointed the commission to study how to honor Mayor Jackson and Mayor Allen.

Campbell went on to say:

Lacking such signals from the top, the argument flowed on. Lots of white people became surprisingly vocal in wanting to keep the name of Mayor William Hartsfield, while lots of black people became surprisingly vocal in wanting to rename the airport after Jackson.

Naturally, I consider my own views deeply rational and color blind, but I also agreed with the herd of white people. Let Hartsfield be Hartsfield. Honor Jackson with fresh memorials.

Yet too many other Atlantans wanted Jackson's name on the city's biggest property. The Jackson Airport campaign got rolling fast after former Mayor Andrew Young said on TV that Jackson deserved nothing less. Jackson's widow, Valerie, then seemed to demand it. Some politicians started arguing that the airport should be named for a black man no matter what the white establishment wanted, and Franklin's committee was in trouble.

Even so, Franklin was expected to endorse her committee's recommendation. Last week, the committee said the airport should keep its Hartsfield name, and a new billion dollar international terminal should be named after Jackson.

That would have been OK with Andy Young, as he'd already made clear. The City Council, though split, would have gone along as well.

But something happened, and Franklin switched. "There's just been so much debate," she said Monday.

So he talked with Young, and she learned that Valerie Jackson would accept a hyphenated

---

16. AJC Editorial Page, Readers Respond, 8-2-2003
17. AJC Editorial Page, Readers Respond, 7-7-2003

Courtesy of Bob McGill © 2012 Shutterbug Atlanta. Current Atlanta FAA tower

airport after all, and on a crazy Friday afternoon she came out for a compromise. [18]

Not one of these officials contacted the Hartsfield family to see if they would be willing to accept a compromise. I think we should have been consulted. I also believe it was a huge mistake by Atlanta's government and I will never be satisfied with their decision.

Campbell's column ended with his guidelines for memorials. The last one read, "And when you name something, do it for centuries, not for 30 years."

the recent move to rename the airport

My letter to the editor appeared in the paper on October 1:

18. AJC, 9-23-2003, p. B2

Obviously, the recent move to rename the airport was not well-received by members of my family, relatives of former Mayor William B. Hartsfield.

We were relieved when the special commission appointed by Atlanta Mayor Shirley Franklin recommended that the name of the airport remain Hartsfield International. But then she recommended to the City Council that the name be changed to Hartsfield-Jackson. Our family felt that this watered down the honor that had been given to Hartsfield.

The Hartsfield family was never against Atlanta's honoring former Mayor Maynard Jackson. We simply felt that the airport already had a name and that it should remain, because of Hartsfield's vision for an international airport for the city and the state.

Atlanta seems to have a bad habit of changing the names of memorials, streets and public buildings, whenever someone else comes

Courtesy of Bob McGill © 2012 Shutterbug Atlanta. Aerial view from FAA control tower

Courtesy of Bob McGill © 2012 Shutterbug Atlanta. Aerial view from FAA control tower

along who was a public figure and worked on a particular project. Without question, Jackson did some good things at Hartsfield, but he simply built on what was already there.[19]

When I was quoted, it was always followed by a disclaimer: Hartsfield, of Acworth, is an advertising sales representative for the ***Atlanta Journal-Contitution***. As of 2006, I am no longer employed by the ***AJC***.

City Council was scheduled to vote on October 20, 2003. It was apparent that the proposed hyphenated name was going to be accepted. Hartsfield-Jackson Atlanta International Airport would become the fifth official name in less than eighty years. C. T. Martin was leading the charge for the City Council to hyphenate the airport name.

D. L. Bennett wrote, "Hartsfield relatives meet, lobby mayor" on Thursday, September 25, 2003, as written below:

> *A few distant relatives of former Atlanta Mayor William B. Hartsfield asked Shirley Franklin on Wednesday to keep Hartsfield's name alone on the city's airport.*
>
> *The Atlanta mayor listened to the five for about an hour. But she wasn't persuaded to abandon her push to rename Atlanta's airport Hartsfield-Jackson International Airport to honor Maynard Jackson, the city's first black mayor.*
>
> *"I'm glad to have had the chance to talk with them," Franklin said. "I understand how hard this is for them. I didn't agree."*
>
> *The family members say they will continue to lobby to protect the name of Hartsfield International Airport.*

19. AJC, Editorial Page, A14, 10-1-2003

Courtesy of Bob McGill © 2012 Shutterbug Atlanta

"We feel the hyphenated name would be watering down the legacy of Mayor Hartsfield," said Dale Hartsfield, 45, an automotive advertising sales representative for the **Atlanta Journal-Constitution**.

"The family's point of view is to keep the name what it has been for 32 years."

Family members don't expect to win but they said they were pleased at least to be heard.

"We thank the mayor for meeting with us," said Hartsfield, whose grandfather was a distant cousin of the six-term Atlanta mayor. "She made some statements we agreed with and some we didn't. Her mind is pretty well made up."

Marsha Hartsfield Hendricks, 49, Dale Hartsfield's sister, said the meeting gave the mayor "something to think about."

"I asked her woman to woman if she would change her mind." Hendricks said. "It's a woman's prerogative."

Dale Hartsfield said family members will meet with the mayor again before the expected Oct. 20 vote by the City Council.

The debate over the airport's name has raged since Jackson's death on June 23. Jackson's widow, Valerie, various elected officials and a large contingent of Jackson supporters have insisted that Hartsfield International Airport be renamed for Jackson, who expanded the hub and gave it international reach.

Many other Atlantans, mostly white, have opposed removing the name of former Mayor Hartsfield, who had the vision of making Atlanta an aviation center.

The family had been largely silent through the

debate, Dale Hartsfield said, because many are private people who didn't want to get involved in a controversy with divisive racial overtones.

Others figured there was no way to win, he said, now it's probably too late, he conceded.[20]

On Monday, October 6, I spoke to the Atlanta City Council at their meeting. They had the ultimate decision on the future name of the airport and I wanted them to hear my views. Following is a transcript of my speech to the Council on Monday, October 6, 2003:

Good morning, distinguished members of the Atlanta City Council. First, thank you for agreeing to hear members of the Hartsfield family on this important issue.

I hope that you will allow me to make my statements uninterrupted. Then, I would love to have an open discussion with you. Why have I taken a stand on this issue?

First, I am a man that truly believes in standing and fighting for what I believe in. I believe in my God, my country, my work, my friends, and my family.

Although I am a distant relative of the late Mayor William B. Hartsfield, I none the less am proud of my family heritage. Mayor Hartsfield loved and was very proud of Atlanta.

Our arguments include: The airport already has a name, why change it? Plain and simple, Mayor Hartsfield fathered aviation in Atlanta. It is thus appropriate that the airport bear his name. Once someone is honored for their

20. AJC, Metro Section C, p. 1-3, 9-25-2003

Courtesy of Bob McGill © 2012 Shutterbug Atlanta. The previous international terminal before 2012

Courtesy of Bob McGill © 2012 Shutterbug Atlanta. Atlanta skyline taken from the FAA tower in 2012

accomplishments, that honor should remain for at least a century. The airport has been called Hartsfield only 32 years.

*I refer to an editorial by the **Atlanta Journal-Constitution's** Cynthia Tucker, on August 6, 2003. Ms. Tucker wrote that renaming the airport would snub history. She said if the airport is renamed, the City will send a message that tribute is fleeting and history anything but sacred.*

Tucker went on to say that it was Hartsfield's vision that boosted Atlanta into leadership as an aviation center. It would be a mistake, a grievous mistake, to deny Hartsfield's accomplishment. Tucker also said in the same article, that mistake would be compounded by a narrow-minded race consciousness, which clearly undergirds some of the support for renaming the airport. Tucker and I ask how did a desire to honor Jackson deteriorate into race baiting.

*Atlanta is an international city. It is a "city too busy to hate." That is a saying that was popularized by then Mayor Hartsfield in the late 1950's. It was Mayor Ivan Allen who had to live up to that saying in the 1960's and Mayor Maynard Jackson who proved it in the 1970's. I got this from a Sunday front page story by Jim Auchmutey, in the **AJC** on July 6.*

*In the **USA Today** story, by Larry Copeland, this past Friday, Copeland said, that this does not look good for the city "to be embroiled in such a fracas."*

If the white community wanted to add a white man's name to a black public figures's honor, that would be unacceptable. So, how is it accepted that the black community could add a black man's name to a white man's honor? That doesn't make sense. Don't let race effect your thought's on this issue. We should be beyond that. I hope that we are. I certainly don't judge a person by the color of their skin. The Hartsfield family also questions why Atlanta has such a bad habit of renaming memorials, street and public buildings. What about a hyphen? A hyphenated name will water down the honor for both men.

I trust that you all have read the letter to Mayor Franklin from Monty Cheshire. I know that he sent it to each of you. Monty Cheshire is William B. Hartsfield only grandchild. He is not here today because he is a very private person, as is a lot of the Hartsfield family.

Monty believes that Atlanta government is thinking too small in honoring Mayor Jackson. You should honor him with a living, breathing organization that carries on his belief's in helping and developing minority education and business development. You have his letter. I trust you will read it if you haven't already.

I was pleased when the Advisory Committee said that honoring Mayor Jackson with a new international terminal and street into said terminal was a fitting tribute for him at Atlanta's airport. You could certainly do that and more.

The Hartsfield family does not have a problem with honoring Mayor Jackson. Atlanta should honor him. But why take away an honor that was bestowed on Mayor Hartsfield?

Courtesy of Bob McGill © 2012 Shutterbug Atlanta

As members of the City Council, have you talked with the people that you represent, white and black? Have you talked with the business community? Are you representing what is best for Atlanta?

The decision is yours to make. Honor Mayor Jackson in a proper way. Don't take away from Mayor Hartsfield's honor in doing so. Regardless of what you decide, I will always introduce myself, as I have since I was a teen, as Dale Hartsfield, like the airport.

After today, I will not make further public comment about this until you have made your decision. You know how we feel.

On October 20, we will know how you feel.

Dale Hartsfield [21]

In 2006, I found the following comments posted on Airlines.net website:

Here's an important part of the airport's history...when they unnecessarily slapped the "Jackson" name on the airport...William B. Hartsfield was a good name, and a good mayor, I don't see what was so wrong with it the way it was.
DeltaGuy [22]

Another comment said:
What annoyed me about it was the way they approached it. If you didn't support Jackson's name on it then you were a "racist" in the "City Too Busy to Hate." Even worse was the way they wanted to rip Hartsfield's name completely off of it. [23]

It is unfortunate that racial tension still exists in our great country. It continues to cause great

21. Transcript of Dale Hartsfield's speech to Atlanta City Council, 10-6-2003
22. www.airlines.net, A Closer look at Atlanta's Airport History, 2-16-2006
23. www.airlines.net, A Closer look at Atlanta's Airport History, 2-18-2006

Courtesy of the Atlanta Hartsfield-Jackson International Airport. New control tower

division and mistrust. We hoped that our first black president would have brought about positive "hope and change." Only history will tell.

The commission also stated that the third recommendation of the commission "could support" the renaming as Hartsfield-Jackson. The report stated that this "… received majority support (a biracial vote of 8 to 7)." Two persons did not vote for this recommendation, and it was not noted if they were the co-chairmen.

In regard to the public forums that were held, it was noted in the commissions report that in session one, "The session was attended by approximately one-hundred people, most of whom were African American." I often wondered, what about Mayor Allen, the white mayor? Sadly, he was mostly ignored.

When the Atlanta City Council voted on the final renaming, October 20, 2003, the voting went mostly by race. The white councilmen voted to keep the name Hartsfield only, while the black councilmen either voted for Jackson's name only or voted to name the airport Hartsfield-Jackson.

On October 20, 2003, the Atlanta City Council voted to change the official name of the airport to Hartsfield-Jackson Atlanta International Airport. As upset as I was with this vote, I was relieved that they did not remove Hartsfield completely. The Hartsfield family would reluctantly have to accept the hyphenated name.

2003 was certainly engaging and challenging, and ultimately, disheartening to many Atlantans and the Hartsfield family.

Courtesy of Bob McGill © 2012 Shutterbug Atlanta. Delta International headquarters at the Hartsfield-Jackson Atlanta International Airport

Chapter Six
The Jackson Era

Maynard Holbrook Jackson, Jr., was born March 23, 1938. He was born in Dallas, Texas, and was the third of six children. His father, Reverend Maynard Jackson, Sr., moved the family to Atlanta when Jackson became the pastor of Friendship Baptist Church in 1945. Maynard was seven at the time. His mother, Irene Dobbs Jackson, was a French Professor at Spellman College in Atlanta.

Jackson was a conscientious student and maintained top grades in Atlanta's segregated schools. In his earlier years, he considered becoming the third generation of Jacksons to become a Baptist minister. However, after entering Morehouse College, Jackson majored in history and politics.

His father died in 1953. John Wesley Dobbs, his maternal grandfather, had great influence on him during his later teen years. Jackson's grandfather was a civil rights leader. Dobbs, recognizing his grandson's oratory skills and intellect, encouraged him to become a lawyer.

Maynard Jackson, Jr., a child prodigy, was 14 years old when he entered Morehouse College in Atlanta. He graduated at age 18, in 1956, with a bachelor's degree in political science and history.

He later attended Boston University Law School for a short time. After several jobs, in 1964, he graduated cum laude from North Carolina Central University law school as a Phi Beta Kappa.

In 1965, he returned to Atlanta as an attorney for the National Labor Relations Board and was admitted to the Georgia bar. He later served with the Emory

Courtesy of the Atlanta Hartsfield-Jackson International Airport

Courtesy of Thomas Nash, portrait artist, with permission from Valerie Jackson

Community Legal Services Center, providing free legal services to low-income Atlantans.

The same year, Jackson married Burnella "Bunnie" Hayes Burke. They had three children, Elizabeth, Brooke and a son, Maynard III, "Buzzy." Maynard and Bunnie divorced in 1976. The 1968 assassination of Reverend Martin Luther King was a turning point in his life. The Dobbs and Jackson families were close friends with Reverend King.

Within months, Maynard Jackson, Jr., launched his first political race, becoming the first African-American to run for statewide office in Georgia since reconstruction, in a campaign he was destined to lose against Georgia's legendary Democratic U.S. Senator Herman Talmadge. Candidate Jackson countered the campaign's racial overtones running ads, "Maynard Jackson doesn't intend to be a 'Negro Senator'. He is dedicated to representing all the people of Georgia." A year later, he successfully campaigned to become Atlanta's first African-American Vice Mayor.[1]

---

1. Maynard Jackson Obit in The Atlanta Journal-Constitution from June 25 to June 28, 2003. See more at: http://www.legacy.com/obituary

Jackson was thirty years old when he ran for United States Senate against the incumbent, Senator Talmadge. Jackson, a democrat, won less than a third of the statewide vote, but carried Atlanta. He instantly became a force to be reckoned with in city politics. He lost the senatorial bid, but decided to seek the position of Atlanta's vice-mayor the following year. He was the vice mayor during the Sam Massell administration. Massell was Atlanta's first and only Jewish mayor.

Carefully planning his campaign for vice-mayor of Atlanta in 1969, Jackson did not take the African American vote for granted. He campaigned tirelessly, appearing in black churches every Sunday until election day. At that time, the black population of Atlanta was approximately fifty percent. He also sought and won one-third of the white vote. Along with ninety-nine percent of the African American vote, he was elected vice-mayor. About the same time, he co-founded and became the senior partner of Jackson, Patterson & Parks, the first black law firm in Georgia's history.

aggressive and outspoken mayor

In 1973, Jackson campaigned successfully against the incumbent Mayor Sam Massell, winning almost sixty percent of the vote. He served three terms as mayor of Atlanta, two consecutive terms and a third term later. He was the 54th and 56th mayor of Atlanta. In his role as mayor, Atlanta went through some difficult transition years from predominantly white leadership to a more even racial power balance. Jackson earned a reputation as an aggressive and outspoken mayor.

Courtesy of Bob McGill © 2012 Shutterbug Atlanta. International gates prior to the new international terminal

MIKE LUCKOVICH'S BEST OF 200[3]

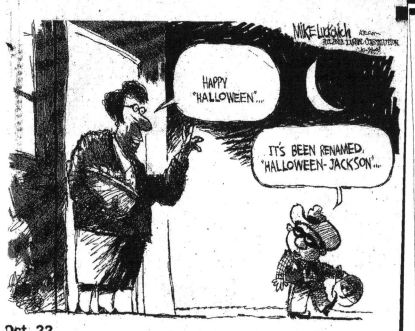
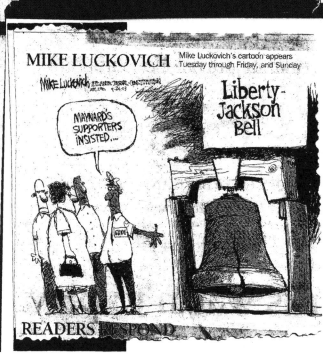

"By permission of Mike Luckovich and Creators Syndicate, Inc." Political cartoons in the Atlanta Journal Constitution created by Mike Luckovich

During his time in office, Jackson's leadership was credited for some great events in Atlanta. Atlanta's rapid rail system, MARTA, was substantially expanded through federal funding during Jackson's tenure. Atlanta was also named the host city for the 1996 Olympics during Jackson's last term in office.

After being elected vice mayor, he presided over the board of aldermen. While Jackson was serving in this role, the charter of the city of Atlanta was modified to strengthen the authority of the mayor. The new charter changed the aldermen to council members and replaced the vice mayor with the position of president of the city council.

Under the new charter, which enhanced the mayor's power, Jackson assumed office in January 1974. He brought in an outside administrator to restructure and reorganize city departments. The administration was centralized and new planning districts were established, with improved neighborhood and citizen input.

In 1974, Jackson was selected to receive the Samuel S. Beard Award for Greatest Public Service by an Individual 35 Years or Under. This award is given annually by Jefferson Awards.

Jackson provoked his first major racial crisis, in May 1974, when he attempted to fire John Inman, the incumbent white police chief. Atlanta's growing crime problem and charges of racial insensitivity toward African Americans, prompted Jackson's decision to fire Inman. The firing increased racial tensions within the city, and detracted from Atlanta's proud motto: "a city too busy to hate," which had first been used by Mayor Hartsfield.

reverse discrimination

Another controversy followed in August 1974, when Mayor Jackson chose an African American college friend, to become public safety commissioner. The new commissioner, A. Reginald Eaves, lacked police experience and created a great deal of controversy when he appointed an ex-convict as his personal secretary. He also put into place a system of quota promotions, and hiring in the police department, which many described as "reverse discrimination."

Courtesy of Thomas Nash, portrait artist, with permission from Valerie Jackson. Photo of Maynard Jackson with Bill Cosby

Courtesy of Thomas Nash, portrait artist, with permission from Valerie Jackson. Photo of Maynard Jackson, former Mayor Andrew Young and Billy Payne, Chief Executive Officer of the Atlanta Committee for the 1996 Olympic Games

Courtesy of the Atlanta Hartsfield-Jackson International Airport. The old and new control towers side by side before demolition of the first mid-field control tower. These towers were 585 ft. apart

Despite the objections Eaves remained in his post, and by the spring of 1976, Atlanta experienced a drop in crime rates. However, Eaves resigned after a police exam cheating scandal was uncovered.

In 1980, Jackson married Valerie Richardson, with whom he had two more children, Valerie and Alexandra.

announced his intention to seek a third term as mayor

In 1989, Jackson announced his intention to seek a third term as mayor of Atlanta, running against Michael L. Lomax, a county commissioner and literature professor at Spelman College. Jackson's eloquent rhetoric and political reputation, proved to be overwhelmingly decisive. Unable to overcome a thirty-four percent point deficit in the polls, Lomax withdrew from the race.

Although both major candidates were black, Lomax had become identified as the "white" candidate, and Jackson the "black" candidate, a decidedly comfortable position in a city where nearly two thirds of the population was black.

As Jackson was cruising toward the October 3rd nonpartisan election, a former black city councilman and civil rights activist, Hosea Williams, emerged late in the campaign to challenge Jackson. William's candidacy gained little support, and Jackson coasted to victory, capturing an overwhelming seventy-nine percent of the vote. One of the losing candidate's strategists put it this way, "Maynard Jackson is god in this town, and how do you run against god?"

In January 1990, Jackson began his new term of office by promising to follow Mayor Andrew Young's footsteps, working with our business community. Mindful of criticism of his predecessor's overly pro-business slant, Jackson promised to devote more attention to the neighborhoods and the problems of the poor in Atlanta.

The Mayor's popularity soared when he helped to secure Atlanta's choice as the site of the 1996 Summer Olympic Games. Several public works projects, such as improvements to highways and parks, and the completion of Freedom Parkway, were expedited in the early and mid 1990's in preparation for the Olympic Games that began in August 1996.

Jackson created an organization to assist students who were academic underachievers to help them develop leadership, self-esteem, and critical thinking skills. During the early 1990's, Jackson also served as president of the National Conference of Democratic Mayors and president of the National Black Caucus of Local Elected Officials.

Courtesy of the Atlanta Hartsfield-Jackson International Airport. August 5, 2006 demolition of the old control tower at Atlanta airport

Courtesy of Bob McGill © 2012 Shutterbug Atlanta. Present day control tower

Chapter 6 - The Jackson Era

Courtesy of Thomas Nash, portrait artist, with permission from Valerie Jackson

Considered a shoo-in for a fourth term as mayor, Jackson stunned supporters in 1993 by declining to run again, citing the effects of a heart-bypass operation, in the fall of 1992. After leaving the mayor's office, Jackson conducted a $12.3 million bond sale for a city-backed apartment project and secured a lease to operate a restaurant and bar at Hartsfield International Airport. Jackson said Atlanta was a "success-oriented city", whose greatest strengths were its people, and its ability to adapt to change. Now the trade and convention hub of the southern states, Atlanta was chosen to host the 1994 football Super Bowl.

Jackson's firm, Atlanta-based Jackson Securities Inc., was named one of the top five black investment companies by ***Black Enterprise*** magazine in 1996. As the chief executive of the company, Jackson was the lead manager for $337 million worth of securities issues and co-manager for $2 billion worth of securities.

Maynard Jackson, Jr., died unexpectedly in June 2003, at the age of 65. He suffered a heart attack during his travels through the Ronald Reagan Washington National Airport. His body would lie in state at city hall and at Morehouse College before a memorial service at the Atlanta Civic Center, which drew more than 5,000 mourners. His was buried at the Oakland Cemetery in Atlanta. In addition to the name changes at the airport, Southside Comprehensive High School in Atlanta was renamed Maynard Holbrook Jackson High School in his honor in 2008.

Jackson's death brought about the controversy in 2003, when the discussion of renaming the airport began to surface. When I began hearing the talk of possibly changing the name of Hartsfield Atlanta International Airport, I knew a battle was brewing. I was in high school when he was first elected mayor in November 1973. I knew very little about his life or political career. I did know that the renaming news was encroaching on my family's history, and I had to be part of this upcoming battle. I would "fight" to keep the airport named for Hartsfield.

what did Jackson do for the airport

What did Jackson do for the airport? One of Mayor Jackson's initiatives during his first and second terms as mayor of Atlanta, was to enhance the services and reputation of Atlanta's airport, by building a new terminal, thus making the airport more modern and accommodating for international travel. The midfield terminal was considered to be Jackson's greatest accomplishment, overshadowing even his efforts to bring the Olympics to Atlanta.

Jackson himself touted the airport reconstruction and modernization as a stroke of great management and government by constantly pointing out that the project had come in both "under budget and ahead of schedule." [2]

2. Quote by Maynard Jackson in 1977. Quoted numerous places including The Atlanta Journal-Constitution and in the Jackson obit

As for the airport and Jackson's race relations, the airport was the key project where Jackson demanded that minority-owned companies be given a fair share of the employment in the construction and remodeling of the airport. Jackson basically indicated that the project would not move forward without appropriate representation from black owned businesses and contractors, or at least joint ventures with white owned companies. Again, many people saw Jackson's insistence upon giving contracts for the airport project to black owned businesses as "reverse discrimination." The project and Jackson's stance on awarding the contracts, served to divide even further the chasm

Courtesy of Thomas Nash, portrait artist, with permission from Valerie Jackson

Chapter 6 - The Jackson Era

between the black owned and white owned businesses in the greater Atlanta community. The employment contracts actually postponed the building of the midfield terminal. However, the success of the project was Jackson's vindication that his approach was the right one.

The reconstruction project at the airport created a lot of racial tension. I believe it would be impossible to be the first African American Mayor of Atlanta, or any southern city, and not be accused of or involved in some type of racial tension. Jackson seemed to provoke many of those tensions, and the airport was a prime example.

Early during his tenure as mayor, Jackson was credited with bolstering race relations in the city through affirmative action plans. His plans dramatically increased business contracts awarded to minority owned companies. On the surface, Jackson was bringing the city together and enhancing race relations, but behind the scenes there was turmoil and scandals.

Toward the end of Jackson's second term in office, the city became the focus of widespread national attention, due to a string of child murder cases in Atlanta. The unsolved murders

Courtesy of Thomas Nash, Atlanta portrait artist. The finished painting of Jackson that was commissioned by Valerie Jackson now hangs in the Jackson International Terminal

Courtesy of Thomas Nash, portrait artist. Nash's studio where he worked on the portrait of Maynard Jackson that was commissioned by Valerie Jackson

threatened to overshadow Jackson's considerable achievements in his first term in office, including the overall downturn of crime and homicides in Atlanta. Jackson played a prominent role in resolving the case, by supporting the Atlanta police and other police forces in the area, but also by endeavoring to quiet the huge amount of public tension that arose because of the serial killings. Wayne Williams, the suspected murderer, was caught in 1981, tried, convicted, and sentenced to serve two consecutive life sentences in prison.

Courtesy of Bob McGill © 2012 Shutterbug Atlanta

his accomplishments as mayor

Barred by the city charter from serving more than two consecutive terms, Jackson left office at the end of 1981. At the end of his second term, Jackson could look back with some pride on his accomplishments as mayor.

Under Jackson's leadership, Atlanta made many gains as a financial center and distribution hub. Expanded international convention amenities turned Atlanta into a major convention center. In 1981, the prestigious Places Rated Almanac named Atlanta the best major city in which to live and work.

As he was leaving office, he established an Atlanta branch office for a Chicago law firm that was strategically positioned for public business. As a bond lawyer with political savvy, Jackson attracted politically connected businesses from many African American mayors and, in the process, enriched himself and his political contacts.

Even between Jackson's first two terms as Mayor in the 1970's and 1980's and his third term in the 1990's, he remained heavily involved in both the political and the business scenes in Atlanta.

In 2003, Jackson's involvement in the Atlanta airport once again involved racial undertones. Even in death, Jackson was claiming a hold on the airport. The renaming process simply meant taking away or diminishing the historical achievements of a white man who had well served as mayor of Atlanta and replacing his achievements and honors in order to honor a black man who had indeed made a tremendous impact on the city. But wasn't there a way to honor one leader without taking away the honor that had already been bestowed upon another leader?

I wonder if things would have been different if the people had been allowed to vote. Obviously, it depended on whether the vote came from the City of Atlanta or the entire surrounding metro area, due to the racial makeup of the areas. The airport served the entire state of Georgia and the southeast.

turn the chapter about Jackson upside down

Ulysses Simpson, a black acquaintance who worked with me at the *AJC*, suggested that I write a book about the controversy of the renaming of the airport. Simpson suggested that in the book, "turn the chapter about Jackson upside down." He also said "to help sell the books, make it controversial." I didn't have to make it controversial, it already was. To present the facts about Jackson and his accomplishments, was enough.

In 2003, I spoke with Mrs. Valerie Jackson at length over the phone during the renaming process. After the renaming was settled at the council meeting, I spoke with her briefly. When the time came to writing my book, I made numerous attempts to contact Mrs. Jackson, but was unsuccessful. I would like to have included her viewpoints.

Maynard Jackson, Jr., received many honors and leadership appointments during a lifetime of public service. He was named by Georgia Governor Roy E. Barnes to the board of the Georgia Department of Industry, Trade and Tourism, serving as chair of the International Trade Committee. He was the founding chairman of the U.S. Conference of Mayors Committee (USCM) on the arts. He also served as the founding chairman of USCM's Special Committee on the Census Undercount.

Maynard Jackson, Jr., was the chairman of the Rebuild America Coalition, founding chairman of the Atlanta Economic Development Corporation, Urban Residential Finance Authority and co-founder of the Urban Residential Development Corporation. He was a member of Fannie Mae Advisory Board, a director of the Georgia Chamber of Commerce and Central Atlanta Progress.

Courtesy of Bob McGill © 2012 Shutterbug Atlanta

Maynard Jackson, Jr., served as chairman of President Jimmy Carter's Local Government Energy Policy Advisory Commission and a vice chairman of the White House Commission on the Windfall Profits Tax. He served as founder, chairman and principal teacher of the Maynard Jackson Youth Foundation, Inc., a trustee of Morehouse College, and a national board member of the NAACP.

Maynard Jackson, Jr., was the first African-American Mayor in Atlanta. Without a doubt that was quite an accomplishment in the south, in the 1980's. He also was the youngest person to ever be elected mayor in Atlanta. His three terms were only eclipsed by Mayor Hartsfield's twenty four years (six terms) as the longest serving mayor of Atlanta. Jackson helped bring the Olympics to Atlanta. His administration was in power when the airport began to grow in leaps and bounds in the 1970's and 1980's. He was the Mayor when the midfield terminal was built. But it was his decision that delayed the building of the terminal with his affirmative action plans, wanting twenty-five percent of the construction companies to be black owned or in a joint venture with white owned companies.

but to name the airport for him

I believe that Mayor Jackson should have been honored, but I do not believe the airport was the appropriate place to add his name. The Atlanta government had suggested naming the new inter-

Courtesy of the Atlanta Hartsfield-Jackson International Airport. At the opening of the 5th runway in May 2006, Steve Penley's painting was unveiled by Mayor Shirley Franklin and Aviation General Manager, Ben De Costa

Courtesy of Bob McGill © 2012 Shutterbug Atlanta. The new Maynard H. Jackson International Terminal at the Hartsfield-Jackson Atlanta International Airport

national terminal for Jackson. I believe that would have been an appropriate honor. International flights had greatly increased while he was Mayor. But to name the airport for him? Considering the accomplishments of Mayor Hartsfield, my family felt like adding Jackson's name to the airport was unjustifiable and undeserved. To the blacks of Atlanta, it was something that should be done. Why? Well, it was to honor their hero, whose administration did modernize the airport and make it grow. I understand that. While the airport continued to grow during Mayor Jackson's three terms, I believe naming rights were taking it a little too far.

I believe the airport would have continued to grow substantially, regardless of who was in office. By then, it was a well-oiled machine!

Background information from "Maynard Jackson: A Biography" By Robert Holmes, Copyright 2011, by Barnhardt & Ashe Publishing

Courtesy of Bob McGill © 2012 Shutterbug Atlanta

Courtesy of Bob McGill © 2012 Shutterbug Atlanta. Photo taken from the Atlanta FAA tower overlooking Delta's jet base and the new international terminal

Courtesy of Bob McGill © 2012 Shutterbug Atlanta. View from the Atlanta FAA tower

Courtesy of Bob McGill © 2012 Shutterbug Atlanta. The Maynard Jackson International terminal in 2012 before the official opening

Chapter 6 - The Jackson Era

Courtesy of Bob McGill © 2012 Shutterbug Atlanta

Courtesy of Bob McGill © 2012 Shutterbug Atlanta. View of world's busiest airport

Courtesy of Bob McGill © 2012 Shutterbug Atlanta

Courtesy of the Atlanta Hartsfield-Jackson International Airport

Chapter 6 - The Jackson Era

Courtesy of Ray Leader, Federal Aviation Administration (Retired), Hartsfield-Jackson Atlanta International Airport. The front of the 1961 Terminal

Chapter Seven

Facts, Figures & Future

Airport Names

CANDLER FIELD
Named for Coca Cola magnet Asa Candler, who also was an Atlanta Mayor from 1916 - 1919.

ATLANTA MUNICIPAL AIRPORT
First named Atlanta Municipal Airport in 1929. The official records were "lost." In 1942, the Atlanta Board of Alderman (later called the Atlanta City Council) had to "re-name" it Atlanta Municipal Airport, because the post office continued to call it Candler Field.

ATLANTA ARMY AIRFIELD
Although never an official name, the U.S. Military called the airport, Atlanta Army Airfield, during World War II. Federal funds were received to help in the airport's growth, because the military used it to service military aircraft.

WILLIAM B. HARTSFIELD ATLANTA AIRPORT
Named in honor of Mayor Hartsfield less than two weeks after his passing in 1971.

WILLIAM B. HARTSFIELD ATLANTA INTERNATIONAL AIRPORT
The airports fourth official name. The word international was added less than six months after being named for Hartsfield because Eastern Airlines started regular international flights in 1971.

HARTSFIELD-JACKSON ATLANTA INTERNATIONAL AIRPORT
Mayor Jackson's name was added to the airport after his unexpected death in the summer of 2003.

ATL
The abbreviated name listed on your baggage claim tickets and the name used by pilots. It has never been an "official" name.

ATLANTA AIRPORT
Most Atlantans still refer to the airport as the "Atlanta Airport." Even after the addition of the Hartsfield and Jackson names, the airport is still known by many as the "Atlanta Airport." After 2003, the media begin to call it by it's official name "Hartsfield-Jackson Atlanta International Airport."

Interesting Facts

Jack Gray was the airport's first manager, from 1929 -1962. He was a visionary and a leader. Along with Mayor Hartsfield, Gray helped to shape the airport that would soon become the busiest airport in the world.

Delta Airlines moved its headquarters to Atlanta on March 1, 1941, a move that undoubtedly helped change the history of the airport.

In the late 1940's, an observation deck was built on top of the post war terminal that helped pay for the terminal's remodeling, another brilliant idea from Hartsfield. At ten cents per person, visitors could watch the airfield activity. The airport collected over $7,500 during the first seven months the observation deck was open. Mayor Hartsfield did not profit from this.

Courtesy of the Atlanta Hartsfield-Jackson International Airport. The building in the background is the 1946 terminal with the observation deck which was Hartsfield's idea. The terminal was used by the army during WWII before the observation deck was added

Important Dates

April 16, 1925
Mayor Walter A. Sims signs a five-year lease on an abandoned auto racetrack, and commits the city to developing the field into an airfield. As part of the agreement, the 287 acres of land is renamed Candler Field after Asa Candler, the Coca-Cola magnet. The infield of the old racetrack had been used as a landing site for many years prior to 1925.

September 15, 1926
Florida Airways delivers mail on the Tampa/Jacksonville/Atlanta route to become the first commercial flight into Candler Field.

October 11, 1927
Charles Lindbergh is given a hero's welcome as he visits Atlanta in his plane the, "Spirit of St. Louis."

Courtesy of Monty Cheshire, grandson of W. B. Hartsfield. Picture of Charles A. Lingbergh given to Alderman Hartsfield after his famous flight, 1927

Courtesy of Ray Leader, Federal Aviation Administration (Retired), Hartsfield-Jackson Atlanta International Airport. 1939 Terminal and control tower

May 1, 1928
Airmail provider Pitcairn Aviation, later known as Eastern Airlines, begins regularly scheduled air service.

1929
In 1929, Atlanta Aircraft Corporation, an aircraft manufacturing company, built aircraft for a short term in Atlanta. Two of the owners were Ernest Woodruff and William C. Wardlaw. Charles Lindbergh said the aircraft was ten years ahead of its time.

April 13, 1929
The city pays $94,400 for the land. Hartsfield said the name changed to Atlanta Municipal Airport in 1929. However, it was still called Candler field into the 1940's.

June 12 1930
Delta Air Service, later known as Delta Air Lines, begins a trial service from Atlanta to Birmingham, Alabama. On June 18, 1930, Delta Air Service made it an "official" permanent route.

December 10, 1930
Eastern Air Transport, formerly Pitcairn Aviation, inaugurates the first continuous passenger service from Atlanta to New York.

July 4, 1934
Delta re-establishes Ft. Worth-Atlanta route, securing it's place in Atlanta's aviation history as the airport's oldest continuous tenant.

March 1939
The airport opens its first control tower. The tower was one of the first used by the CAA. In December 1941, Atlanta's tower was converted to federal operations, which marked the beginning of the FAA. The tower cost approximately $27,000 to complete.

October 1940
Atlanta airport was declared an air base by the United States Government. Candler Field would double in size during World War II. Although not an official name, the military called the airport Atlanta Army Airfield.

1941
Delta Air Services moved company headquarters from Monroe, Louisiana, to Atlanta. Delta records were lost in a flood, so the exact reason for the move is unclear. The Hartsfield family has always said that Mayor Hartsfield helped to convince Delta to move it's headquarters to Atlanta.

1942

In July, because of a dispute with the post office due to missing records, the city reaffirmed the name was Atlanta Municipal Airport. Mayor Hartsfield was later quoted that he clearly remembered the city officially changing the name in 1929.

During the war years, Atlanta's airport almost doubled in size. In 1942, a record 1,700 arrivals and departures, were recorded in a single day. The Atlanta Airport was named the nations busiest in terms of flight operations.

July 1944

Southern Airlines completes a new $100,000 hanger. At the time, it was believed to be the nation's largest hanger. Southern announced they had planned to start passenger travel as early as 1941.

May 9, 1948

Airport officials were making plans to build a larger terminal, so they temporarily moved operations into a war-surplus hangar. More than one million people came through Atlanta's airport in 1948. The observation deck was the most popular feature. The airport recouped more than half of its $15,000 construction costs, from paying observers, during the first seven months of operation.

Courtesy of the Atlanta Hartsfield-Jackson International Airport

Courtesy of Ray Leader, Federal Aviation Administration (Retired), Hartsfield-Jackson Atlanta International Airport. Terminal 1961 through 1980

1948
Ground-breaking begins as the existing runways are expanded to lengths of 6,000 feet, 6,000 feet, and 7,200 feet. Delta spends more than a million dollars to expand Delta headquarters and maintenance shops in Atlanta. Airplanes had become more commonplace during WWII, but more than three-fourths of the countries population had not flown in 1948.

1957
Work begins on new terminal to help alleviate congestion. Atlanta was the busiest airport in the country with more than two million passengers passing through in 1957. Atlanta became the busiest airport in the world, between the hours of 12 noon and 2 p.m. each day.

May 3, 1961
Atlanta Municipal Airport is ushered into the "Jet Age" with the opening of the largest single terminal in the country. The new $21 million structure could accommodate six million travelers a year. Within its first year, 9.5 million people visited the terminal, visitors and passengers, stretching the new terminal beyond its capacity.

Chapter 7 - Facts, Figures & Future

1964
The Atlanta Region Metropolitan Planning Commission (ARMPC) does the first formal planning studies and proposes the mid-field terminal concept that would open in 1980.

February 1971
William B. Hartsfield dies on Feb. 22, 1971. On Feb. 28, one day before what would have been Hartsfield's 81st birthday, the airport name is changed to William B. Hartsfield Atlanta Airport, thanks primarily to Mayor Sam Massell.

Courtesy of Ray Leader, Federal Aviation Administration (Retired), Hartsfield-Jackson Atlanta International Airport. The old terminal closed in September 1980 and the tower was demolished on July 1, 1984 to make way for the fourth runway

Courtesy of Ray Leader, Federal Aviation Administration (Retired), Hartsfield-Jackson Atlanta International Airport. Atlanta Hartsfield airport control tower opened in 1961

July 1, 1971

The name is changed to William B. Hartsfield Atlanta International Airport, when Eastern Airlines introduces flights to Mexico and Montego Bay, the airport's first continuous international service.

January 1977

Construction begins on the world's largest terminal complex. This $500 million project would be the largest construction project in the south.

June 1, 1978

Sabena Belgian World Airlines becomes Atlanta's first foreign international carrier when it begins service to Brussels four times a week.

Chapter 7 - Facts, Figures & Future

Courtesy of Ray Leader In 1979, Space Shuttle Enterprise, mounted on top of a specially-modified 747, stopped overnight in Atlanta for refueling and cargo checks. Enterprise was a test shuttle, it never went into space. The Atlanta Airport is not suitable for landing a re-entering space shuttle

June 1979

The NASA Shuttle Enterprise mounted on a specifically modified 747, stopped overnight in Atlanta for refueling and cargo checks. The Enterprise never actually went into space. Atlanta airport is not suitable for landing or reentering a space shuttle.

September 21, 1980

William B. Hartsfield Atlanta International Airport opens the world's largest air passenger terminal complex, covering 2.5 million square feet. The terminal is designed to accommodate up to fifty-five million passengers a year.

December 1984

A 9,000 foot fourth parallel runway was completed. A separate expansion the following spring gave the airport an 11,889 foot runway, capable of handling the largest commercial airplanes in use or in development.

June 18, 1988

MARTA's airport station opened, linking the airport to Atlanta's rapid transit system.

September 1994

The new 1.3 million square foot International Concourse E opens. It is the largest, single international facility in the nation. Concourse E is designed to help move international passengers quickly and smoothly to their next destination.

May 1996

The $250 million Hartsfield Improvement Program (HIP "96) is completed. This ambitious renovation and restructuring effort was designed to make Hartsfield a more user-friendly airport. One of the more dramatic improvements of this program is the addition of the beautiful, three-story, 250,000 square feet atrium.

June 1996

The Department of Aviation begins developing its new master plan, "Hartsfield, 2000 & Beyond."

Courtesy of the Atlanta Hartsfield-Jackson International Airport. MARTA rapid transit at the airport

Chapter 7 - Facts, Figures & Future

Courtesy of the Atlanta Hartsfield-Jackson International Airport. Atlanta Airport welcomes the 1996 Olympics

July 1996
The Centennial Olympic Summer Games was a major international multi-sport event that took place in Atlanta, Georgia, from July 19 to August 4, 1996. A record 197 nations took part in the Games, comprising of 10,318 athletes. Airport travel was greatly increased in 1996.

February 1999
Hartsfield gains the title "World's Busiest Airport" in passenger volume after accommodating 73.5 million travelers in 1998.

March 2000
Hartsfield is recognized as the "World's Busiest Airport" in terms of both passenger traffic, after accommodating more than 78 million passengers and more than 900,000 departures and arrivals for 1999.

April 2001
The City of Atlanta celebrates the ground breaking for the new fifth runway at Hartsfield. This project is a major component of the $6 billion-plus, 10-year capital improvement program. Other

projects include a new international terminal and Consolidated Rental Car facility (CONRAC). The fifth runway is the largest public works project in Georgia history.

October 2001
Following the attacks of 9/11, enhanced security measures were adopted at the nation's airports. Members of the Georgia National Guard begin security patrols at Hartsfield to support existing security personnel and Atlanta police officers at Hartsfield.

October 2003
To honor late Atlanta Mayor Maynard H. Jackson, Jr., the Atlanta City Council votes to add his name to the airport's existing name. Hartsfield-Jackson Atlanta International Airport recognizes the visionary leadership that both William B. Hartsfield and Maynard Jackson, Jr., had for the airport. Hartsfield-Jackson, the world's busiest passenger airport for the fourth consecutive year, stands as a testament to two of the city's greatest leaders.

Courtesy of the Atlanta Hartsfield-Jackson International Airport. 5th Runway Project

Courtesy of the Atlanta Hartsfield-Jackson International Airport

July 2004

Construction begins on the $215 million TSA Baggage Security Screening Project, which creates specially constructed rooms below the airport roadways for explosive detection systems currently located in the ticketing lobbies. As part of the project, additional screening facilities were constructed at International Concourse E, airport roadways were re-configured, and improved terminal curb fronts were installed.

December 2004

A record 83.6 million passengers passed through the airport, and since 1998, Hartsfield-Jackson has retained its title as the world's busiest passenger airport. Additionally, a record 6 million international passengers travel through Hartsfield-Jackson, marking a 103 percent growth since the city of Atlanta hosted the 1996 Olympic Summer Games.

July 2005

Hartsfield-Jackson celebrates its 80th birthday. From its humble beginnings to its present world class distinction and into its illustrious future, the airport continues to be a vital link in the world's air transportation system.

May 2006
The fifth runway opens. It is hailed as "The Most Important Runway in America." Dale Hartsfield, the author of *What's In A Name?*, is among the passengers of the first plane to take off and land on the runway.

January 2007
Hartsfield-Jackson receives several prestigious national honors. It was named "Best Large U.S. Airport" by *American Express Executive Traveler Magazine*. It was named "Most Efficient Airport in the World" by Air Transport Research Society. General Manager Ben De Costa was named "Best Airport Director" by *Airport Revenue News Magazine*.

February 2008
Forbes Magazine names Hartsfield-Jackson the No. 1 airport in the nation for Wi-Fi connectivity

Courtesy of Bob McGill © 2012 Shutterbug Atlanta

March 2009
Hartsfield-Jackson Concessions program wins the ***Atlanta Business Chronicle*** "Best in Real Estate: 2008 Deal of the Year Award" in the retail category. Hartsfield-Jackson receives ***Airport Revenue News*** "2009 Best Concessions Management Team Award."

April 2009
Ben De Costa, Aviation General Manager, named "Man of the Year" by ***Atlanta Tribune***. Hartsfield-Jackson's cargo operation receives "Award of Excellence" by ***Air Cargo World***.

May 2009
Hartsfield-Jackson was recognized "Airport of the Year" by ***Air Cargo Week***. Airport appoints Milton M. Castillo, as its first chief financial officer.

June 2009
The Air Transport Research Society recognizes Hartsfield-Jackson with its "Award of Excellence for Efficiency."

July 2009
Hartsfield-Jackson sets a world record for monthly flight operations (88,408).

October 2009
Alaska Airlines begins service at Hartsfield-Jackson. Aviation General Manager, Ben De Costa, is appointed to the Airports Council International World Governing Board.

November 2009
The Airport's new dog park opens.

Hartsfield-Jackson receives the "Airport Safety Mark of Distinction Award" from the Federal Aviation Administration Southern Region, Airports Division.

The Airport's Concessions unit wins the "Airports Council International–North America's Best Convenience Retail Program Award" in the large airport category, and the 2009 Concessions Person of the Year (Director of Concessions).

December 2009
Hartsfield-Jackson's new rental car center and ATL Sky Train opens to the public.
Hartsfield-Jackson Chief Information Officer, Lance Lyttle, is named to the 50 Most Important African-Americans in Technology list by eAccess Corp., a San Francisco-based publisher.

May 12, 2012

Opening of the Maynard B. Jackson International Airport. This cutting-edge, LEED-certified (Leadership in Energy and Environmental Design) facility is the new global gateway through which travelers from throughout the world connect with more than 150 U.S. cities. For those traveling from the United States, the international terminal is the gateway to nearly 80 destinations in more than 50 countries.

Current Runway's (2014)
1. 9R-27L = 9,000 feet long (2,743 meters). Category III
2. 9L-27R = 11,889 feet long (3,624 meters). Category I
3. 8R-26L = 10,000 feet long (3,048 meters). Category II
4. 8L-26R = 9,000 feet long (2,743 meters). Category III
5. 10-28 = 9,000 feet long (2,743 meters). Category II

Terminal Complex

The terminal complex measures 130 acres, or 6.8 million square feet. The complex includes the

Courtesy of Bob McGill © 2012 Shutterbug Atlanta. Maynard B. Jackson International Terminal

domestic and international terminals building and concourses T, A, B, C, D, E and F. Within these concourses, there are a total of 207 gates comprised of 167 domestic and 40 international gates. The airport is free of any architectural barriers to people with disabilities.

Airport People Mover

The airport's underground Automated People Mover connects all concourses with the domestic and international terminals and consists of eleven, four-car trains operating on a 3.0 mile loop track. Trains operate approximately every two minutes. On average, the trains carry more than 200,000 passengers per day.

Parking

There are more than 30,000 public parking spaces at Hartsfield-Jackson, including over 10,000 in covered parking decks. Special parking spaces are also provided for disabled passengers in each lot. Parking at the international terminal is easy and convenient. Two new parking facilities provide more than 3,500 spaces within minutes of the international terminal.

Courtesy of Bob McGill © 2012 Shutterbug Atlanta. Hotel adjacent to airport holding area

Courtesy of Bob McGill © 2012 Shutterbug Atlanta

International shuttle connector
Atlanta-bound passengers cannot access secured areas of the airport after they pick up their luggage at the international terminal baggage claim, so the airport has established shuttle services to link passengers at the international terminal with existing facilities. The international shuttle connector offers direct service from the international terminal to two locations including the rental car center.

Rental Car Center
In December 2009, Hartsfield-Jackson opened a convenient, state-of-the-art, 67.5 acre facility that houses all rental car company operations and vehicles. The rental car center includes two four-story parking decks, more than 8,700 parking spaces, and a 137,000 square foot customer service center. The rental car center features 13 rental car agencies - Advantage, Airport, Alamo, Avis, Budget, Dollar, Enterprise, E-Z, Hertz, iTravel, National, Thrifty and Payless Rent a Car companies.

ATL SkyTrain
Connecting customers to the rental car center is a new elevated train, dubbed the ATL SkyTrain. In five minutes, passengers are connected to the rental car center, the Georgia International Convention Center, and hotels and office buildings. The train operates six two-car trains which can carry 100 passengers and their baggage.

MARTA
The Metropolitan Atlanta Rapid Transit Authority (MARTA) provides train and bus service to the metro Atlanta area. MARTA's Airport Station connects to Hartsfield-Jackson at the west end of the domestic terminal building between Domestic Terminal North and Domestic Terminal South baggage claim areas.

Chapter 7 - Facts, Figures & Future

Concessions

There are 263 concession outlets throughout the airport, 114 food and beverage locations, 90 retail and convenience outlets, three duty-free stores and 56 service outlets, including a banking center, a U.S. Postal service, Georgia Lottery outlets, a shoe shine, ATMs, vending machines and spas. Concessions space covers approximately 230,000 square feet.

Cargo

There are three main air cargo complexes, North, Midfield and South, a Perishables Complex and a USDA Propagated Plant Inspection Station. The total on-airport air cargo warehouse space measures 29.8 acres or 1.3 million square feet. There are 28 parking positions for cargo aircraft, 19 at the north complex and 9 at the south complex

Employment

Hartsfield-Jackson is the largest employer in the state of Georgia. There are over 58,000 airline, ground transportation, concessionaire, security, federal government, City of Atlanta and Airport tenant employees.

Courtesy of the Atlanta Hartsfield-Jackson International Airport

Courtesy of the Atlanta Hartsfield-Jackson International Airport

Economic Impact

Hartsfield-Jackson has a direct economic impact of more than $32.5 billion for the metro Atlanta area economy every year.

Passenger data

Hartsfield-Jackson Atlanta International Airport official passenger data from October 2013 year to date shows that 78,197,408 passengers passed through the airport, with 55,099,035 of them being passengers of Delta, Atlanta's largest carrier. These figures are actually down 1.34% from the same period in 2012.

The Future

In 2007, The FAA completed an update to the original 2004 study that determined which airports in the United States "would have the greatest need for additional capacity in the next twenty years." (FAA FACT 2 Study)

"The Atlanta metropolitan area and Hartsfield-Jackson Atlanta International Airport (ATL) was identified as needing additional capacity. Based on these findings, the FAA initiated the Atlanta Metropolitan Aviation Capacity Study (AMACS) in 2008 to explore the methods and means by which short and long-term aviation capacity in the metropolitan Atlanta region could be enhanced."

Therefore, the airport will have to be continuously improved and perhaps a "reliever" airport can also be built. Eight sites in the greater metro area have been considered in recent years with over twenty nine sites actually looked at.

The eight final site locations are:
Dawson/Forsyth (Greenfield Site)
Cherokee County Airport
Cartersville Airport
Cobb County Airport – McCollum Field
Barrow County
Paulding Northwest Atlanta Airport
Dobbins Air Reserve Base
Gwinnett County Airport – Briscoe Field

Courtesy of Dale Hartsfield 2012

Courtesy of Bob McGill © 2012 Shutterbug Atlanta. Federal Aviation Administration building

Although no one can predict the future, I have some closing thoughts about the airport's future.

Based on the history of the airport and the management by the City of Atlanta, will the airport name change again? Probably! I personally would prefer the Atlanta city government officials consider the history of the airport, and rightfully return it to, what I believe it should be called, Hartsfield Atlanta International Airport! One of the major purposes in writing ***What's In A Name?,*** was to show that Mayor Hartsfield was the "Father of Aviation" in Atlanta, and to defend why the airport should solely bear his name!

Facts and figures were obtained from www.atlanta-airport.com, the official website of Hartsfield-Jackson Atlanta International Airport. For more indepth information about the airport, go to: www.atlanta-airport.com. Other sources include: "A Dream Takes Flight" by Betsy Braden & Paul Hagan.

Courtesy of Bob McGill © 2012 Shutterbug Atlanta

Courtesy of Bob McGill © 2012 Shutterbug Atlanta

Chapter 7 - Facts, Figures & Future

Courtesy of Bob McGill © 2012 Shutterbug Atlanta

Courtesy of Bob McGill © 2012 Shutterbug Atlanta

Made in the USA
San Bernardino, CA
05 May 2017